Haiku Journey
Through 20th Century Music

Haiku Journey
Through 20th Century Music

Dave R. Muñoz
(Haiku Dave)

SUNCLOUD PRESS
Battle Groound, WA, USA

Suncloud Press
www.suncloudpress.com
1406 SW 5th Avenue
Battle Ground, Washington 98604
USA

Copyright ©Dave R. Muñoz (Haiku Dave) 2019. All rights reserved.

Printed in the United States of America. All rights reserved. No part of this publication may be reproduced, distributed or transmitted in any form or by any means, without prior written permission except in the case of brief quotations in articles of reviews. For more information please contact Suncloud Press.

Haiku Journey Through 20th Century Music
Library of Congress Control Number: 2019910799

ISBN 978-0-9905328-3-5

First Printing: November 2019

Book and cover design by Jim Shubin, www.BookAlchemist.net

Editor and Publisher : Cristina Olsen, Suncloud Press
Artwork: © Dave R. Muñoz (Haiku Dave)
Front cover photography: © Cristina Olsen
Back cover author photograph: © Cristina Olsen

Dedication

To my wife Cristina who has both literally and figuratively saved my life more than once.

Acknowledgements

This book wouldn't be possible without the support of the following people:

My late beloved grandmother, Anna Maria Romero, and my parents, Jessie and Albert Muñoz for their faith and love.

Doug Ogden and family, Maria Lynn Santamaria and Cristina de Santamaria Graff, Sherill Flint, Taylor Tan, Jennie and Jonathan and Aspen Hinman, Clarice Stasz, Elizabeth Jaffe, Jeanette Mcclendon, Anne and Dougie Zesiger, Cleveland Justis, Marjorie Sennett, Jim and Patricia Swanson, Patricia Taylor and Burr Snider, Qi Zeng, Naomi Gibbs, Barbara Fillips, Kevin Tripp, Miguel Rae and family, Beverly Cherner, Ralph Muñoz, Jennifer and Brian Sturgeon, Mark Klinkkammer, Steven Riffkin, Celestine Gebrier, Sheila Singleton, Jackie and Brian Titus, Sheryl Cardoza, Steve Tabak, Nathaniel Emmert-Keaton, Mike Morrison, Robin Purcell, Colleen Dolan, Catherine John, Glyn Peterson, Jennifer Daly, Dr. David Rahdert, Dr. Eric Franklin Tepper, Dr. Tanya Zamorano.

And for Lynn and Truman of the Golden Cream Doughnut Shop in San Rafael, California for years of great treats and kindnesses on my way to work.

With deep appreciation!

Introduction

The concept for this book first started as a simple idea. I wanted to create one hundred years of haikus inspired by my beloved songs and instrumentals from the 20th century, my way of sending a 'love letter' to many of my favorite composers, artists and performers. Since 2001 I have anticipated creating such haikus by listening, singing, dreaming and whistling to them, all straight out of my music library! And library it is—as the chosen pieces indeed come from CDs, vinyl, and old 78-rpm discs. My personal music collection consists of a full spectrum of music genres and styles from the volatile 20th century.

My haikus are presented in chronological order, an instrumental and a song for each year, starting with the year 1900. I loosely base each decade by thematic-style and history of that specific era. Each haiku is accompanied by an "optional reading" for those of you interested in the social and historical context of the songs.

The format of a traditional Japanese haiku consists of three lines of 17 syllables, divided into 5, 7, 5 syllable lines. While I adhere to the 17-syllable format, I diverge from the syllabic line rule and add another component that is rarely found in haikus: rhyming and occasionally an acrostic (first letter of each line forming a word).

An accompanying CD with all the music celebrated here would have been ideal—but also costly. Maybe for another edition, if lady luck will have it. However, I encourage you to search on the internet for the songs and instrumentals that inspired me to create such haikus. They are all available in varying editions on CD, vinyl, and through YouTube and other online digital media. I also encourage you to look up certain years you may have a personal connection to the year of your birth, the year of a major event, a family member or friend's birthday. . .Enjoy the entertainment and the musical education.

Haiku Instrumental 1900

Mist clears over the sound—
here on shore's ground
where ocean and tales abound.

Inspired by *Piano Concerto no. 2 in c-minor, op.18* by Sergei Rachmaninov. This is the pinnacle of Rachmaninov's work, straddling the fence between Classical music's Romantic and Modern eras. I am often moved by both the sheer beauty of this piece and the yearning it evokes for the preservation of the Old Century as the world shifts into an unimaginable New Century.

Haiku Song 1900

Songbird stung by a bee,
was it gold's allure
or the promise of honey?

Inspired by "Bird In A Gilded Cage" by Arthur J. Lamb and Harry von Tilzer. The song is about a newly wedded wife in the hands of a wealthy money mogul. This theatrical song served as a counterpoint to the Morgans and Rockefellers of the Industrial Revolution, indicating that all that glitters isn't gold. Of the two versions that were published in 1900 my favorite is Jere Mahoney's on brown wax cylinder, Edison Records. This theme of a trapped gold digger appears many times throughout the 20th century, the 1975 Eagles song "Lyin' Eyes" being a great example.

Haiku Instrumental 1901

"Grandma, where do rivers end?"
"Take my hand . . .
I'm the delta, you're the sea."

Inspired by *Symphony no. 2 in D-Major, op. 43* by Jean Sibelius. Much like Rachmaninov, Finish-born Jean Sibelius also found himself on the fence between the Romantic and Modern eras. *Symphony no. 2* is dear to me as it pays homage to one of my favorite composers of the Romantic Era: Johannes Brahms, especially the finale of Sibelius' last movement.

Haiku Song 1901

Roses bloomed,
come home soon
so I may wear you like my favorite perfume.

Inspired by "I'll Be With You When The Roses Bloom Again," a staple of Country music artists. I first heard it sung by Johnny Cash. I later discovered that the Will D. Cobb and Gus Edwards 1901 song was written in Tin Pan Alley, a music publisher district in New York City that produced almost every known song from the 1880s to circa 1964.

Haiku Instrumental 1902
Park Pigeons I

Park pigeons
serve as painters
on statue heads of past entertainers.

Inspired by "The Entertainer" by Scott Joplin, taken off a piano roll. The Acoustic Era (1890 to 1922) was not kind to the piano, as it did not pick up audio very well. The great Ragtime composer Scott Joplin was never recorded on a phonograph. However, his sheet music and piano rolls became extremely popular at the turn of the century, and Ragtime would prevail to later become one of the main ingredients in Jazz, just a decade away!

   Scott Joplin would have his day 71 years later. In 1973 film composer Marvin Hamlisch revived "The Entertainer" for the motion picture The Sting featuring Robert Redford, Paul Newman, and Robert Shaw.

Haiku Song 1902

After harvest
trucks will haul off grapes
taking with them long summer days.

Okay, I'm cheating already! Inspired by two songs: "When The Harvest Days Are Over" composed by Howard Graham and Harry von Tilzer, and "In The Good Old Summer Time" composed by Ren Shields and George Evans. Both songs are in the style of the male Barber Shop quartet, popular in the Acoustic Era.
    Because no electricity was utilized at that time, recordings were fed through a large horn into a foil vibrating reed cutting into the wax cylinder or record discs, hence making many instruments difficult to be heard clearly, like the piano, violin, string instruments, and guitar. Mainly hard sounding instruments were recorded, such as brass bands like John Phillip Sousa's. It was either big horns or big vocals, and vocal recordings were preferred.

Haiku Instrumental 1903

"You hear the trombone?
It says: don't be alone,
and dancing's good for bones."

Inspired by "American Beauty Waltz (Music For Trombone)" by an anonymous composer, performed and recorded by the Columbia Band on Oxford Records. At the turn of the 20th century "parlor music" was at its height. Salon folk would gather to hear storytellers, poets and mood music to set the ambiance of the gathering. The trombone soloists of this charming instrumental play the waltz with great fun and humor, goading the listeners to move their bones . . . ever-so-slightly.

Haiku Song 1903

Silver beams
through a gold sunset . . .
alchemy over Earth's canopy.

Inspired by "Silver Threads Among The Gold," originally composed in 1873 by Eben E. Rexford and Hart Pease Danks for sheet music and parlor songs. The song resurfaced in popularity from 1902 to 1915 with the advent of the phonograph. This type of overly sentimental ballad was popular in this era. In this song the balladeer husband pronounces his eternal love, sung by the amazing Acoustic Era tenor Henry Burr.

Haiku Instrumental 1904

. . . didn't see
the Statue of Liberty
but I did see sycamore trees.

Inspired by the banjo duet "By The Sycamore Tree Medley" by Vess L. Ossman and W.P. Hunter. In the Acoustic Era the banjo was supreme over all string instruments. For starters the staccato picking of string instruments made it possible for the banjo to be heard above the acoustic recording horn. Ossman and Hunter were master banjo players, much like putting Eric Clapton and Jimi Hendrix together to record this tour de force of Ragtime syncopation . . . and it was only 1904!

Haiku Song 1904

Let's meet at the World's Fair
so I may win your heart
or a teddy bear.

Inspired by the song "Meet Me In St. Louis, Louis." I've loved this song from the moment I heard the last line of the 1944 motion picture *Meet Me in St. Louis* where Judy Garland happily says, "I can't believe it…right here where we live, right here in St. Louis!" I was hooked at nine-years old! The song was composed by the New York team of Andrew B. Sterling and Kerry Mills. As it happened one night, the two were in a bar and one of the drinks was named "Louis," and by chance the bar tender working that evening was also named "Louis." As the drinks came so did the song, "…I'll have another Louis, 'Louis'" and history was created. The song was released July 1904 during the World's Fair in St. Louis, Missouri, known as the Louisiana Purchase Exposition, one of the greatest social events of the 1900s. The Fair showcased our ever-growing interest in electricity (still a novelty at the time), mesmerizing visitors with lights illuminating buildings and Fair roadways. The song was sung by Irish singer Billy Murray known as "The Denver Nightingale."

Hug a Teddy Bear Lately?

Did you know that the teddy bear was created in honor of President Teddy Roosevelt? Out on a bear hunt with some cronies, Teddy hadn't found a single bear. So his assistant decided to corner one in a hollow tree and invite him to shoot it. But Teddy refused, seeing this as a very unsportsmanlike behavior. A maker of stuffed toys saw a cartoon depicting this event and decided to make a stuffed bear dedicated to Teddy Roosevelt, hence the "Teddy Bear" first made in 1902.

Haiku Instrumental 1905

Washing my face—
drainpipes like sirens
luring my tired skin out to sea.

Inspired by *La Mer* (The Sea) by Claude Debussy. The entire piece consists of three movements. Yet rather than introducing a different theme for each movement, he simply supplied a recurring melody, a precursor to the hypnotic music of Ravel and even later Ambient music of the second half of the century: mysterious, mesmerizing, and at times rapturous.

Haiku Song 1905

I dozed off as you read
Newton's book . . .
I had the apple coming.

Inspired by "In The Shade of The Old Apple Tree." Written by Harry H. Williams and Egbert Van Alstyne, it was thought to be inspired by an apple tree in Central Park; yet there were no apple trees in the park. Regardless of the mystery of the apple tree, this sentimental ballad was sung by Henry Burr for Edison Records on cylinder.

Haiku Instrumental 1906
Nursery Rhyme

In Paradise Garden
child devotes time and seeds
to await good deeds.

Inspired by *The Walk To The Paradise Garden* by Frederick Delius. English-born, musically German-taught, and a disciple of French Impressionism, just days before his opera premier of *A Village Romeo And Juliet*, Delius added "*...Paradise Garden*" as an interlude. As history would have it, the opera did not fare well, however "*...Paradise Garden*" became one of his greatest triumphs.

Haiku Song 1906

"She loves me—she loves me not . . ."
Wind takes my daisy . . .
"Could be she loves me?"

From Racial Grief to Redemption

Inspired by the song "Nobody," composed by Bert Williams and Alex Rogers. "Nobody" was one of the most popular songs in the Acoustic Era, and one of the funniest. My whimsical haiku honors co-composer and African American singer, legendary Bert Williams. Williams was born in Nassau, the Bahamas, to a black mother and Dutch father, and moved to the U.S. when he was 11 years old. Williams had an innate talent for comedy and acted in vaudeville and minstrel shows, except for one catch: being the only black man with a stage troupe of all white members, the lightly-skinned performer often was made to wear black cork polish over his skin and to mimic the "black man."

    Racial conflicts played a significant role in William's life, but he rose above them becoming one of the greatest entertainers of the 1900s and 1910s. And yet, while audiences applauded his genius, they politely denied him social rights. His friend, film comedian W.C. Fields, once said of him, "Bert was the funniest man I ever saw, and the saddest man I ever knew."

    With "Nobody," composed for the Broadway Musical *Abyssinia* in 1906 and recorded by Columbia Records, Williams brought down the house and topped the best seller list. In the song, Williams plays the hard-luck character that he would play for the rest of his career. The song's longevity is due to its outright comedic tone. In 1910 Williams joined the *Ziegfeld Follies* until 1919. He was only 47 when he died in 1922, in conjunction with the demise of the Acoustic Era. During the second half of the 20th century Bert Williams' song would be recognized as a masterpiece and would go on to receive numerous music history awards—and rightly so.

Haiku Instrumental 1907

Living years in evergreen
till shades of maple
added more life scenes.

Inspired by "Maple Leaf Rag," composed by Scott Joplin (1899), recorded on October 15, 1906 by The U.S. Marine Band, aka The Washington Military Band, and issued on disc in March of 1907. Scott Joplin's compositions were highly influential and "Maple Leaf Rag" became a masterpiece due to its variety in tone, melody and outright catchiness! "Maple Leaf Rag" would also go on to be one of the most recorded works of the 20th.

Haiku Song 1907

When windstorms
throw me in a malaise
I think of you and school days.

Inspired by "School Days (When We Were A Couple of Kids)." It was one of the first school-themed songs ever recorded, creating a perfect blend of playfulness and nostalgia. Composed by the team of Will D. Cobb and Gus Edwards, who also composed "I'll Be With You When The Roses Bloom Again," which inspired my Haiku Song (1901). However, "School Days" became their signature song. It sold several million copies of sheet music and in 1907 was the best-selling record of the year. My favorite line in this song is the misuse of scholastic fundamentals, "Readin' and 'ritin and 'rithmetic…"

Here is a brief list of "school songs" currently rolling around in my scholastic brain:

Chuck Berry – "School Days"
Paul Simon – "Me And Julio Down By The Schoolyard"
The Ramones – "Rock 'n' Roll High School"
Pink Floyd – "Another Brick In The Wall (Part II)"
Steely Dan – "My Old School"
Supertramp – "School"
Alice Cooper – "School's Out"

Haiku Instrumental 1908

I see fall cotton dust
make a snow-like drift . . .
as if winter's waiting.

Inspired by *Gaspard de la Nuit* (for solo piano) by French composer Maurice Ravel. French composers from as early as the Baroque Period had been mastering the art of *program music*. In the Romantic Period, composer Hector Berlioz brought the art form to a national height with *Symphonie Fantastique* (1830). Many of these musical works were based on plays, ancient stories, mythology, paintings, and poems. Ravel's *Gaspard de la Nuit* is based on a set of three poems by Aloysius Bertrand, telling a story of goblins and nightly creatures, much in the vane of his contemporary Edgar Allan Poe. Of the three movements, my favorite is the first one, "*Ondine*," telling the tale of the water nymph Undine who lures her victims to the bottom of the lake with her song. Here is a brief list of some of my favorite French composers of *program music*:

Hector Berlioz (1803–1869) / Charles Gounod (1818–1893)
Camille Saint-Saëns (1835–1921) / Leo Delibes (1836–1891)
Gabriel Fauré (1845–1924) / Claude Debussy (1862–1918)
Paul Dukas (1865–1935) / Erik Satie (1866–1925)
Maurice Ravel (1875–1937)

Haiku Song 1908

" . . . She went to a baseball away-game."
"How long has she been gone?"
"Eight years."

Inspired by two songs: "Take Me Out To The Ball Game" and "She Forgot To Bring Him Back." Along with the "Star Spangled Banner," few can forget "Take Me Out To The Ball Game," written by the great Tin Pan Alley team of Jack Norworth and Albert von Tilzer and sung in every baseball park in the country from April to October for over 100 years. In October of 1908 the song hit the bestseller list with the Haydn Quartet featuring the grand Billy Murray.

    Marriage as a subject matter was a popular song theme in 1908 and many were hilarious! My personal favorite is the great goddess of the Acoustic Era, Ada Jones, singing "She Forgot To Bring Him Back" with great comedic gusto. Written by William McKenna (and possibly May Irwin, music), it was released March 1908 on Edison wax. It is a tale of an overly trusting wife who discovers her husband is overly interested in her neighbor. It's been one of my biggest dreams to one day see a live performance of this charming song.

Haiku Instrumental 1909

At times I imagine
peace from within
trusting bliss deep in my skin.

Inspired by *Symphony no. 9 in D-Major* by Gustav Mahler. This would be the last complete symphony by the world's fleeting great Late Romantic Period composer. Mahler would not live long enough to witness the "Classical" music genre take a huge shift into the "Modern" music style. Mahler died in 1911, just two years short of witnessing Igor Stravinsky change the direction of Classical music to another musical universe with his premiere of *Le Sacre du Printemps* (The Rite of Spring). Gustav Mahler's *Symphony no. 9* gave his audiences a dramatic tale of life, death and transcendent bliss, finishing his astonishing great career at the doorstep of the 20th century where music and human civilization would radically change.

Haiku Song 1909

Silver dollar moon,
shine bright over my field.
If it rains—rain pennies!

Inspired by "Shine On, Harvest Moon," composed by Jack Norworth and his wife Nora Bayes in late 1908. Nora went on to perform this great composition, yet I have never heard a recording of Nora singing her trademark song. However, in 1909 many artists recorded this seminal song, none better than by the king and queen of vaudeville, Billy Murray and Ada Jones, in May of 1909. Recorded on Edison Records, the song stayed on the top seller list for over a month, taking it to the moon!

Nora Bayes and Ada Jones shared their diva status to great heights in the Acoustic Era. As a young man in 1978 I fell in love with Nora Bayes and I placed her photo in my bedroom. My mom once exclaimed, "Dave, she would be just perfect for you if she hadn't been dead since 1928!" My reply was, "Mom, it's all relative."

Haiku Instrumental 1910
Park Pigeons II

Bronzed archer –
eyes on prey, fingers on bow,
pigeons sit on cocked elbow.

Inspired by *Firebird Suite (1910 First Version)* by Igor Stravinsky. In 1910 the suite premiered for Diaghilev's *Ballets Russes*. By 1945 Stravinsky would rework the ballet three more times. It tells a story of Prince Ivan who falls in love with a princess, telling a wonderful tale of innocence versus evil. The 1910 *Firebird* gave the Late Romantic audience what they wanted to hear: dramatized music with tonal imagery.

Haiku Song 1910

Life's a train
which pulls us like a chain
till we get off and ride again.

Inspired by "Casey Jones." This legendary train song based on a true event has been beloved by popular and folk music artists for a century. Composed by T. Lawrence Seibert and Eddie Newton, it tells the story of John Luther Jones, aka Casey Jones. Casey was a railroader who died tragically in April of 1900 on the Cannonball Limited out of Memphis. He had attempted to save his passengers by stopping his train from colliding with a stalled freight train. Casey became a tragic hero after finding his body in the wreckage with fused hand still on the throttle-handle. In 1910 the American Quartet featuring Billy Murray made this record a top seller. Throughout the 20th century many versions of "Casey Jones" have been sung, including one by the Grateful Dead in 1970.

Haiku Instrumental 1911

Gently rowing
on a raft upstream
like a bow on violin strings.

Inspired by *Summer Night On The River* by Frederick Delius. We've already encountered Delius in 1906 with *The Walk To The Paradise Garden*. Here my haiku pays homage to his love of the violin. This composition was conceived in the garden of Fontainebleau. Listen closely to the footsteps of small stream animals, gnats and water-spiders surfing the flowing water. And if you are hard of hearing, look and picture the riverside paintings of Monet, Pissarro, Whistler, and Sisley.

Haiku Song 1911
Berlin Has Arrived!

Birds leave their trees
as marching bands pass through . . .
children climb up for a view.

The Birth of America's Songwriter!

Inspired by "Alexander's Ragtime Band," Irving Berlin's first hit, my haiku insinuates marching bands passing through town to announce that "Irving Berlin has arrived!" Written when he was 23 years old, his genius was already evident, and his influence on a mass of budding composers was monumental (Gershwin, Porter, Rodgers, and Arlen). Berlin would give birth to hundreds of songs and live to 101-years old! In 1942 he would create one of the highest selling recordings in our country's history . . . but you'll have to wait until I take you to 1942.

Haiku Instrumental 1912

"You hung up red peppers
for mistletoe."
"I know you wanna hot kiss!"

Inspired by "Red Pepper (A Spicy Rag)" by Fred Van Eps (King of The Banjo), successor to Vess L. Ossman (the reigning banjo king). Van Eps masterminded note phrasing, especially bending notes which would become essential in the Blues, and for all guitar players alike. Again, listen closely to how "parlor music" of the day interweaves with ragtime as Van Eps and eight musicians play a wild dance tune displaying evidence of things to come... Jazz!

Haiku Song 1912
The Titanic

Released a firefly
to glide far and free
till she vanished out at sea.

Inspired by "The Firefly," based on the 1912 operetta and title song by Otto Harbach. On April 15, 1912 the ill-fated maiden voyage of the Titanic symbolized the end of an era. The massive and hasty output of the Industrial Age led to the tragic sinking of the Titanic and begged the question: what is the price of progress on the human spirit when, like Sisyphus, we roll the Great Rock uphill time and time again only to have it crash down time and time again?

Haiku Instrumental *Le Sacre du Printemps*

Dark amber clouds flow . . .
a blanket of snow—
my foot awakes earth below.

My foot summons fall leaves . . .
each step tells where they've been
and where they're going.

Inspired by *Le Sacre du Printemps* (The Rite of Spring) by Igor Stravinsky. On May 29, 1913, at the Théâtre des Champs-Élysées, Paris, a young Russian composer set free a ballet work that would forever change the music world–setting forth a sort-of metaphorical map to the landscape of the 20th century. *Le Sacre du Printemps* was primitive, folk oriented, and expressive—enough to cause a riot on that fateful night. And yet we listened! With *Le Sacre du Printemps* we did not require a full understanding of Classical music theory, for it broke with all conventions, springing fully formed from Stravinsky's forehead, much like Athena born fully armored from Zeus.

Haiku Song From a Lonesome Pine

You talked pre-med, physics,
and law till you juggled pinecones . . .
then I fell!

Inspired by two songs: "The Trail of The Lonesome Pine," composed by Ballard MacDonald and Harry Carroll, as sung by Henry Burr and Albert Campbell. And "You Made Me Love You (I Didn't Want To Do It)," composed by Joe McCarthy and James Monaco, and first sung by Al Jolson (considered the greatest singer from 1912–1932). My favorite female version of "You Made Me Love You" is Judy Garland singing the tune to a photograph of Clark Gable in the 1937 film *The Broadway Melody*.
    Here is a brief "star struck" list of you-made-me-love-you-and-I-can't-understand-just-what-happened-to-me! love songs rolling 'round in my head:

Rodgers and Hart (composers) – "Bewitched, Bothered And Bewildered" (1940)
Nat King Cole – "You Call It Madness (But I Call It Love)" (1944)
Chet Baker – "It Could Happen To You" (1958)
Peggy Lee – "Fever" (1958)
Johnny Mathis – "Misty" (1959)
Ella Fitzgerald – "Misty" (1960)
Patsy Cline – "Crazy" (1961) (composed by Willie Nelson)
The Lovin' Spoonful – "You Didn't Have To Be So Nice" (1965)
Spiral Starecase – "More Today Than Yesterday" (1969)
Queen – "You Take My Breath Away" (1976)
Jackson Browne – "Ready Or Not" (1973)
Tom Waits – "I Hope That I Don't Fall In Love With You" (1973)

Haiku Instrumental 1914

I gave time,
poems and renderings,
yet you were but a lark ascending.

Inspired by *The Lark Ascending* (1914 version) by British composer Ralph Vaughan Williams. I've loved this lyrical piece since my youth. It's filled with deep English romantic overtones combined with hidden spiritual echoes from the Far East...yet without being sappy. What thrills me most is the violinist playing ever so gently between solos and orchestra, a perfect backdrop for the recitation of Victorian poet George Meredith's poems of nature, love, life and the human experience, for example, his Dirge in Woods:

A wind sways the pines,
      And below
Not a breath of wild air;
Still as the mosses that glow
On the flooring and over the lines
Of the roots here and there.
The pine-tree drops its dead;
They are quiet, as under the sea.
Overhead, overhead
Rushes life in a race,
As the clouds the clouds chase;
      And we go,
And we drop like the fruits of the tree,
      Even we,
      Even so.

Haiku Song 1914

Diamonds are gallstones,
stardust are fleas,
been that way since you *done* left me.

Inspired by "St. Louis Blues." African American W.C. Handy composed "St. Louis Blues" in 1914. Books have been written regarding this masterpiece and it remains one of the most recorded blues song in history. By the 1910's decade ragtime music was spreading everywhere and elements of it were running like race horses in Tin Pan Alley. Publishing houses and the "Popular" songs of the day were dropping hints of the syncopated sound (accenting the upbeat) that would become ubiquitous in Jazz. Handy took it further, weaving ragtime music with the spirituals of human suffering to create the Blues.

Haiku Instrumental 1915

"What's better
than edible flowers?"
(... It's you I long to devour...)

Inspired by *Nights In The Gardens of Spain* by Manuel De Falla. When you first listen to this you might think the instrumental is a piano concerto or a symphonic impression for piano and orchestra, but it's actually a symphonic poem, a colorful soundscape of Spain's landscapes. The three nocturnal pieces within *Nights In The Gardens of Spain* suggest a Moorish Mid-Eastern feel with the Flamenco guitar interweaving an encompassing canvas.

Haiku Song 1915

Is it you
twirling free
or am I dreaming by elusive palm trees?

Inspired by "Down Among The Sheltering Palms," composed by Abe Olman and James Brockman, it became a hit in 1915 as performed by the Lyric Quartet. I first heard this sentimental ballad as a student at San Francisco State University in the late 1980s. It tells a charming story of two divided lovers: he on the East Coast and she in the Bay Area. The song appears many times in Hollywood musicals: *That Midnight Kiss* (1949), *Some Like It Hot* (1959), and *Down Among The Sheltering Palms* (1953).

Haiku Instrumental 1916

Fountain forms
an armillary sphere—
I jump in to tie the Cosmos.

Inspired by both *Fountains of Rome* by Ottorino Respighi and "Jupiter" from *The Planets, op. 32* by Gustav Holst (completed 1916 and premiered 1918).

    In *Fountains of Rome Respighi* created a pastoral symphonic poem inspired by four Roman fountains in the course of a day (ending the beautiful work at nightfall). On October 6, 2012 my wife Cristina and I got to hear *Fountains of Rome* performed at the San Francisco Symphony and as the music played I conceived the draft of this haiku.

    "Jupiter" from Gustav Holst's symphonic poem *The Planets* tells a celestial tale of our Solar System from the viewpoint of seven planets. "Jupiter" is my favorite of the symphonic poems. What thrills me most about "Jupiter" is how Holst brought in hints of Sir Hubert Parry's song "Jerusalem," also composed in 1916 (which served as a coronation anthem in England).

Haiku Song 1916

I'm no fool—
smart chimps use tools,
yet when dancing
I bruise my wife prancing.

Inspired by the very funny song "I Can Dance With Everybody But My Wife." Composed by John Golden and Joseph Cawthorn (also sung by Cawthorn). This very witty and funny song could easily have been written in an Irish pub. It was first performed by Cawthorn on Broadway in the musical *Sybil*. The song also became famous because of its lightning-fast vocals. (Cautionary note: amateurs who attempt to sing this may bite their lips and bleeding may ensue.)

Haiku Instrumental 1917

At a fork with my faithful horse,
I am in doubt
yet she knows the course.

Inspired by "Livery Stable Blues" by The Original Dixieland *Jass* Band (ODJB), recorded February 26, 1917 in New York on Victor. This is the tune that ignited full blast the smoldering embers of Jazz. For the first time Jazz reaches a mass audience. It is an infectious piece, so catchy to the ear it jumps right down to your dancing toes! A novelty tune with Nick LaRocca's cornet mimicking horse sounds and other farm animals, it is as American as apple pie (or gumbo). Just four years after Stravinsky changed the music world with *The Rite of Spring*, ODJB, which consisted solely of white males, would do the same for Jazz by taking much of the credit for the *birth of Jazz,* but under deceptive circumstances. For in 2017, a hundred years after the recording, music historians found ODJB's claim to be inaccurate, having deprived the African American artists their true glory as the first creators of Jazz.

    There are two recorded examples of African American music artists creating Jazz before ODJB's "Livery Stable Blues": Europe's Society Orchestra's "Down Home Rag" recorded on December 29, 1913, and Wilbur C. Sweatman's "Down Home Rag" recorded on December 1916. Both versions were originally composed by Sweatman. The 1916 version, recorded just two months before "Lively Stable Blues," is clearly *Jazz* with essential blues notes and hopping syncopation!

Haiku Song 1917

Where's this place of fair air
Where angels dare?
If you care, help over there!

Inspired by "Over There." Written by George M. Cohan, it became one of America's most popular anthem-like war songs of World War I. Two years before, the first American anti-war song was released, "I Didn't Raise My Boy To Be A Soldier." Yet on April 6, 1917 the U.S. declared war on Germany. With "Over There" Cohan created a masterpiece. It is musically structured to raise you physically and emotionally out of your seat. The politically minded Nora Bayes sang the song on Broadway bringing down the house with applause, cheers, and many tears, and in November took the record to best-seller status for three weeks... amazing indeed!

Haiku Instrumental 1918

"Grandma, I brought peanuts
for circus tigers."
"ROARRR!"
". . . I'll eat them myself."

Inspired by "Tiger Rag" ("Hold That Tiger") by The Original Dixieland Jazz Band. (By 1918 the group had changed their name from "Jass" to "Jazz.") A few years later lyrics were added to the instrumental, and in 1931 the African American vocal trio The Mills Brothers took this lyric version to great heights, hence creating a huge "Hold That Tiger" craze!

Haiku Song 1918
A Swanee Lullaby One

Rock-a-bye
    to a Swanee lullaby
        floating south
            to the gulf's mouth.

Inspired by "Rock-a-Bye Your Baby With A Dixie Melody," composed by Sam Lewis, Joe Young and Jean Schwartz. In late 1918 the musical-comedy *Sinbad* was sweeping New York's Broadway. The production ran well into 1919 with staggering popularity. The star was early great singer Al Jolson who brought down the house with "Dixie…" and forever left a mark in the American songbook and singers of Southern themes. The musical *Sinbad* would later feature a song just as famous, if not more so than "Dixie…," and that song would be "Swanee" (see Haiku Song 1919).

Haiku Instrumental 1919

Your fingertips
are like a fly-fisher
on my body of water.

Inspired by "Barcarolle" circa 1919, composed and performed by R. Nathaniel Dett. Mr. Dett was a greatly respected African American college music professor, composer and pianist. He taught in black colleges throughout the South and in 1919 he was asked to have one of his pieces recorded for a Boston-based record label. The Barcarolle was originally a musical form that was popular among the Venetian gondoliers (from *barca*, "boat"). In classical music the most famous barcarolles are from Jacques Offenbach's *Tales of Hoffman* and Chopin's *Barcarolle In F-Sharp Major*. And yet, I find Dett's "Barcarolle" to be a deeply moving piece, melancholic to the deepest core, and stunningly beautiful.

Haiku Song 1919
A Swanee Lullaby Two

At Swanee's shore
    from a rock-a-bye dream
        life I've seen
            will flow downstream.

Inspired by "Swanee," composed by Irving Caesar and George Gershwin. Before this masterpiece appeared in the 1920 production of *Sinbad*, Al Jolson had heard "Swanee" preformed in late 1919 to a lukewarm audience. Jolson however saw something different in this upbeat catchy tune. He would interpolate "Swanee" into *Sinbad* and create a phenomenon! Both "Rock-a-Bye Your Baby With A Dixie Melody" and "Swanee" would become synonymous with Al Jolson. Later, "Swanee" would be Gershwin's first major breakthrough in his short yet astonishing musical career.

Haiku Instrumental 1920

Removing their Sunday hats
they whisper
about the wild sermon.

Inspired by "Whispering," a fox trot for dancing composed by John Schonberger and performed by Paul Whiteman and His Ambassador Orchestra. "Whispering" ushered a new type of dance style, mixing Acoustic Era Parlor-Salon music with a little ragtime and a lot of African American Jazz. This debut recording would create a sensation, selling an astonishing two-million copies.

Haiku Song 1920

Me, crazy?
Playin' cards with autumn leaves
with butterflies up my sleeves.

Inspired by "Crazy Blues," composed by Perry Bradford and performed by Mamie Smith. With the Acoustic Era closing in on itself, popular music was evolving as Jazz and Blues slowly began crossing over into a mainstream "white" listening market. In 1920 three record companies dominated the market—Victor, Columbia, and Edison—yet other companies were producing discs for African American artists and selling them to limited distribution. On December 11, 1920 all that changed as Mamie Smith hit the record charts with "Crazy Blues" on Okeh Records. This was a major step for Mamie Smith, one of the first African American artists to cross over to influence a popular audience. The African American floodgate of musical artists could no longer be contained!

Haiku Instrumental 1921

Kitten sleeping on the piano keys—
it jumps
leaving us d-sharp.

Inspired by "Kitten On The Keys" performed and composed by Zez Confrey. "Kitten…" came to him while visiting his grandmother and her kitten jumped on the piano. It became his trademark tune.

Haiku Song 1921

Grandma knitting said,
"it's just silver yarn-thread . . .
soon I'll have your blanket."

Inspired by "Look For The Silver Lining," composed by the team of Bud De Sylva and Jerome Kern, one of the most uplifting songs ever written. In April of 1921 the amazing "white" singer Marion Harris of both Blues and Popular Song fame released "Look For The Silver Lining," which was also used as one of the songs in the popular Broadway musical *Sally*. The musical remained one of the most long-running shows of the 1920s.

Haiku Instrumental 1922

You kiss like champagne—
your body's a sea lane . . .
do it again . . . amen.

Inspired by George Gershwin's instrumental version of "Do It Again!" It was first featured in the Broadway smash hit *The French Doll* with actress Irene Bordoni. Because of its usage of light-hearted double-entendres it was considered too risqué for frequent airing over the newly invented radio. However, its popularity has endured throughout all these years, both as an instrumental and with lyrics.
I've loved this classic George Gershwin piece since I was twelve years old when I first heard Judy Garland sing it in her honeyed voice, making me tingle all over inside (...and because my haikus are rated PG-13 in this book, I must leave it at that).

Haiku Song 1922
Mr. Shean's Canteen

"It's hot Mr. Gallagher."
"Yes, Mr. Shean."
"Yet, hide, hide the canteen."

Inspired by the comedy song "Mister Gallagher And Mister Shean," composed and performed for the *1922 Ziegfeld Follies* by Ed Gallagher and Al Shean. This high tempo Prohibition Era song consisted of the singers giving each other quick, silly, and witty one-liners.

Haiku Instrumental 1923

"Grandma,
how did segregation end?"
"Let's start at the estuary."

Inspired by "Chimes Blues" by Joe "King" Oliver and performed by King Oliver's Creole Jazz Band, featuring a young New Orleans musician, Louis Armstrong, on cornet and the very gifted Johnny Dodds on clarinet.

    Oliver's recordings in 1923 were nothing less than a miracle! For one, all musicians were African Americans in a "white man's recording industry." Second, Lil Hardin on piano was the only woman in an all-male group. And thirdly, this was Louis Armstrong's first solo, blowing on his cornet with the force, eloquence and passion not heard since. Not least, with the end of the Acoustic Era, the group was swept up by the record labels' hungry demand for the "new" Jazz experience. King Oliver's band birthed a genius and clearly the entire 1920s decade would come to symbolize Armstrong, much like The Beatles influenced and symbolized the 1960s.

Haiku Song 1923
A New Era

"I'm down hearted
just as I started, with no cash—
my date departed."

Inspired by "Down Hearted Blues," composed by Alberta Hunter and Lovie Austin, and sung by early Blues legend Bessie Smith—three African American women conjoining their creative talents to produce a masterpiece. By 1923 Columbia Records was heading toward bankruptcy due to a changing listeners market and the advent of radio. Through an act of fate, Columbia signed on Bessie Smith who had been performing sensational sold-out shows around the Philadelphia area. Many music historians believe this African American Blues artist saved Columbia Records from ruin.

Haiku Instrumental 1924

Yes, there are points of view,
shades of blue,
yet I'm drawn to photos of you.

Inspired by *Rhapsody In Blue*, composed by the great George Gershwin. This is the year both Classical and Jazz forms married and opened a parade of music in the American psyche. There is so much I could say about this piece, but since much has already been written, I will simply emphasize three points: 1) *Rhapsody In Blue* is among the first "instrumentals" to receive many music awards; 2) it helped "legitimize" the Jazz genre for a predominately white music-buying market; and 3) it introduced the European Classical composers to Jazz.

My favorite version of *Rhapsody In Blue* is the 1924 version of Paul Whiteman's Concert Orchestra featuring George Gershwin himself on piano.

Haiku Song 1924

Give me back time with you—
as if Earth were new
and we had tea for two.

Inspired by "Tea For Two," composed by Vincent Youmans (music) and Irving Caesar (words), as sung by Marion Harris. Late one night Youmans introduced a piece of music to Caesar, who penned some quick "dummy" lyrics as he was trying to get to bed. Next morning Youmans and Caesar found, much to their surprise, that the dummy lyrics worked very well with the music. "Tea For Two" became one of the most popular recorded songs of the first-half century and one of the most popular piano tutoring songs of the world! Not bad for a "dummy lyrics" song.

Haiku Instrumental 1925

Our day starts
with fresh new magnolia scent
coming from an old tree.

Inspired by "Sweet Georgia Brown" by Ben Bernie and His Orchestra. In 1925 novelty bands were at their height and the emergence of Jazz added a spice of edginess to their joyful sounds. "Sweet Georgia Brown" is a classic, catchy tune guaranteed to have you whistle it all day. It is was so popular that the legendary basketball team The Harlem Globe Trotters used it as their theme song.

Haiku Song 1925

"Grandma,
is hail pounding our roof?"
". . . Oh, it's just fascinating rhythm . . ."

Inspired by "Fascinating Rhythm," composed by George Gershwin (music) and his brother Ira Gershwin (words). The words produced by Ira perfectly complemented the syncopated rhythm of George's Jazz sound, creating a crossover gem that wove together Jazz and popular styles. My favorite versions are performed by Cliff "Ukulele" Edwards, the brother and sister team of Fred and Adele Astaire; and for the fun of it, see tapper Eleanor Powell's breath-taking performance.

Haiku Instrumental 1926

Pouty boy
off to accordion lesson
mumbles, "... dead man walking."

Inspired by "Dead Man Blues" by Jelly Roll Morton's Red Hot Peppers. Composed by Morton, one of the great early Jazz pioneers of New Orleans.
    Death couldn't be more fun! The piece opens up with a funny instrumental "dialogue" that I imagine goes something like this: "It's twelve-noon and the church bells ringin' ... someone must be dead." Then another musician replies, "yeah, dead drunk." Then "Dead Man Blues" starts with a Chopin-like funeral arrangement as the great Kid Ory on trombone leads into an "after burial" march in a dance-like dirge. In 1874 Saint-Saëns composed *Danse macabre,* a popular satirical dirge; you can almost see the skeleton bones of Saint-Saëns jingle in a sing-along jubilee along with "Dead Man Blues," truly one of the most brilliant works to come out of New Orleans, on Victor Records.

Haiku Song 1926
Louis Armstrong

Is that Mom and Pop
dancin' to Jazz,
or do they have heebie jeebies?

Inspired by "Heebie Jeebies," composed by Boyd Atkins and performed by Louis Armstrong and his Hot Five. It was recorded February 26, 1926, one of many great moments in the life of Louis Armstrong. Legend has it that as the Hot Five were playing along in the studio, the sheet music fell off the stand and Louis, not knowing the complete lyrics, began to sing "Heebie Jeebies," employing for the first time the technique of scat singing.

Throughout the history of music there have been "visionary immortals" responsible for altering a genre and taking it into a new direction, such as Bach, Mozart, Beethoven, Brahms, and American 19th century composer Stephen Foster. Louis Armstrong is among the first of the "immortals" of the 20th century. Countless books have been written about his genius, musicianship, and life. Though not the sole inventor of Jazz, Armstrong laid the first Jazz bricks down in New Orleans, then built the jazz scaffolding in Chicago and New York City, and finally completed the rooftop of our country's home of Jazz. For me, many of Louis Armstrong's songs encompass experiences of the human spirit, as listed here:

The river of life: "Riverside Blues" (1923, Armstrong with King Oliver's group).
Never stop dancing: "Heebie Jeebies" (1926).
Never stop being in a state of awe: "Potato Head Blues" (1927).
Never stop seeking enlightenment: "West End Blues" (1928).
Misbehave once in a while: "Ain't Misbehavin" (1929).
Be aware of human suffering and the human endeavor: "Black and Blue" (1929).
Never stop looking deeply into the cosmos: "Stardust" (1931).
Love and be loved: "All of Me" (1932).
Be willing to compromise: "What A Wonderful World" (1968 and re-charted 1988).

Haiku Instrumental 1927

On ship skinning potatoes—
I did fine,
till I had talks with them.

On ship skinning potatoes—
I did fine,
till they had talks with me.

Inspired by "Potato Head Blues" by Louis Armstrong. Groundbreaking events took place in the 1920s: the arrival of the radio era, Jazz, The Blues, Country Music, the Charleston dance, speakeasies, Wassily Kandinsky, F. Scott Fitzgerald, Ernest Hemingway—and lastly, on May 10, 1927 Louis and his Hot Seven recorded one of the greatest music pieces of the 20th century. Treatises have been written on this early masterpiece. "Potato Head Blues" featured one of Armstrong's dearest friends, Johnny Dodds from the "King" Oliver days. Dodds takes the first solo on clarinet frolicking with joy and keeping the listener in suspense, then after a few banjo bars follows Armstrong with one of the finest trumpet solo moments in Jazz history. Within its three-minutes every note is perfectly executed, raising the bar for many other great Jazz artists to follow suit.

Haiku Song 1927
River Suite

"Grandpa,
river's rising from bad weather!"
"I'll be your boatman's tether."

"Sleep grandpa,
eternity's gate runs downstream
so your tired soul may dream?"

"Son,
hear the pounding of the paddleboat?
That's your great-grandpa's heartbeat."

Inspired by "Ol Man River" from the 1927 musical *Showboat*, composed by Jerome Kern and Oscar Hammerstein II, the production was inspired by the Edna Ferber novel of the same name and staged by Florenz Ziegfeld. The musical showcased relationships between blacks and whites on the Mississippi river boat, *The Cotton Blossom*. The show became one of the greatest musicals of all time. With echoes of Dvorak's "Largo" theme from his *"New World" Symphony No. 9*, combined with the heartbeat of the Southern spiritual, "Ol Man River" was sung by the great African American singer Jules Bledsoe (later sung by Paul Robeson in the 1936 production of *Showboat*).

Haiku Instrumental 1928

If you're man enough
to seize the day
you're man enough
to sing ballads.

Inspired by Louis Armstrong's "West End Blues." Composed by Oliver Williams complete with music and lyrics, Armstrong however recorded the tune avoiding all the words and verbally singing the ballad as his voice transformed into a clarinet lullaby. Scat singing had arrived onto the world at large and the father of the craft had brought it home! This quiet masterpiece was released near autumn of 1928 on Okeh Records just as the weather was about to change, and just before the greater tsunami that would take place with The Great Stock Market Crash of 1929.

Haiku Song 1928

Bayou wild flower from Lafayette,
is it love?
Though we haven't met.

Inspired by two songs: "Wildwood Flower" as performed by The Carter Family, and "Lafayette" as performed by Joseph Falcon. Since the advent of radio, over 1,000 stations were broadcasting music and all of America was listening in. Programming became sparse as stations fought for quality shows. By the mid-1920s stations were beginning to invite local musical artists to show up and perform. American Roots music like Cajun, Blues, and Country music flourished. By 1928 Country artists like Jimmy Rogers, Gene Autry, and the legendary Carter Family were making waves in the South. "Wildwood Flower" first appeared in the mid-19th century, but it was the Carter Family that made it famous. To this day, "Wildwood Flower" remains one of the most beloved of American songs.
In 1928 a New Orleans store-owner and friend of Joe Falcon begged Columbia Records to record Joe and his wife Cleoma Breaux's rendition of "Lafayette." It instantly became a sensation, one of the first Cajun songs to be recorded and heard over the radio, and both Falcon and Breaux went on to have a remarkable career. Caution: listening to Joe Falcon may cause spontaneous two-step dancing.
A few of my favorite Falcon tunes are: "Lafayette" (1928); "The Waltz That Carried Me To My Grave" (1928); "Poche Town" (1929); "When I Left Home For Texas" (1929); "La Fille Oncle Elair" (1934); "Le Valse De Madam Sosten" (1934).

Haiku Instrumental 1929

I dip and dance with a broom—
caught again
as your laughter fills the room.

Inspired by "Market Street Stomp" by The Missourians. This wonderful recording with its playful title is hailed as a raucous and flirtatious stomp. The members were based in St. Louis and entertained in this region in the style of the "Roaring Twenties" craze in the East Coast. It was issued just prior to The Great Stock Market Crash of October 29, 1929. How could such a party end? Yet end it did!

Haiku Song 1929

You sing in the rain—
how silly and campy . . .
oh goodness, I'm in love!

Inspired by the song "Singin' In The Rain" from the 1929 motion picture musical *Hollywood Revue of 1929*. Composed by Arthur Freed and Nacio Herb Brown, and performed by major Follies star Cliff "Ukulele" Edwards, whose spirited rendition created a joyful smash. With talkies in its infancy, Hollywood drew audiences in with the thing everybody loved the most: musicals. Hollywood talkies became a sensation, as not everyone could make it all the way to New York City to see a show on Broadway. Now they could simply go to their local theatre and see a musical via film! Fast forward to the 1952 film *Singin' In The Rain* where singer-dancer Gene Kelly slowed the tune down and created one of the greatest dance routines of the 20th century.

Haiku Instrumental 1930

I've seen white snow
and red Bordeaux
yet you're an elusive indigo.

Inspired by "Mood Indigo" by Duke Ellington and His Orchestra. On October 17, 1930 Ellington and his orchestra recorded this masterpiece on Brunswick Records. There are always methods and musical theories to describe pieces of music, yet with "Mood Indigo" one can listen by sense of touch, starting with silk, then warm clay, to silky hair…

Haiku Song 1930

"Gramps, how did you work a sickle all day?"
"Swing right, body—
swing left, soul . . ."

Inspired by "Body And Soul," one of the greatest songs to meld Blues and sentimentality. Composed in 1930 by Johnny Green, Edward Heyman, Robert Sour, and Frank Eyton, it immediately became a sensation in Europe before heading back to the U.S. in the late 1930s to re-create a phenomenon. If you listen closely to "Body And Soul" you can also hear undertones of it in a 1931 masterpiece of Casablanca fame, "As Time Goes By." For fun, here is a brief list of my favorite versions of "Body And Soul":

Ruth Etting (1930)
Annette Hanshaw (1930)
Billie Holiday (1940)
Billy Eckstine (1949)
Ella Fitzgerald with Nelson Riddle (1962)
Tony Bennett and Amy Winehouse (2011)
Coleman Hawkins (instrumental version 1939)
John Coltrane (instrumental version 1961)

(Note: "Body And Soul" also re-appears in Haiku Instrumental 1939.)

Haiku Instrumental 1931

If I see star dust,
I'll make a wish—
if it's satellites, they'll have to do.

Inspired by the 1931 version of "Stardust" by Hoagy Carmichael as performed by Isham Jones & His Orchestra on Brunswick Records. In 1927 Hoagy conceived his masterpiece while visiting his alma mater University of Indiana. As he was walking through campus, he remembered his old college sweetheart and fragments of "Stardust" began playing in his head. He quickly found a piano to compose the work right there on campus grounds! It's thrilling to know where or how great works of art are born . . . like dropping stardust on that very spot.

(Note: "Stardust" also re-appears in Haiku Instrumental 1951.)

Haiku Song 1931

House furniture in sheet covers
read like stories
of bygone lovers.

Inspired by "As Time Goes By," composed by Herman Hupfeld for singer Rudy Vallée. In 1931 the song went unnoticed and would incubate for eleven years before it resurfaced in 1942, playing a major part in the musical landscape of one of Hollywood's greatest motion pictures, *Casablanca,* starring Humphrey Bogart and Ingrid Bergman, with Dooley Wilson singing at the piano. The song has become an American institution. Go to any U.S. city park where *Casablanca* is showing on a large screen under twilight skies and you will witness two things: hundreds of people reciting the film's dialogue and hundreds more singing "As Time Goes By."

Haiku Instrumental 1932

"Dad, why do bright sunsets
never last?
I don't wanna grow up too fast."

Inspired by *Concerto in d-minor for Two Pianos and Orchestra* by Francis Poulenc. By 1932 few Classical composers were creating works within the standard sonata style, yet French composer Poulenc gave us a concerto with three movements (allegro/largo/allegro) to honor the great Classical masters of the past. My favorite part of the concerto is the second movement, larghetto, with beautiful hints of French composer and colleague Camille Saint-Saëns, and a noticeable homage to Mozart's *Piano C Major Concerto, K. 467* (known as the *"Elvira Madigan"*).

As a personal side note, my reference to "Dad," marks my father's birth year of 1932, and the reference to "bright sunsets" goes to one of my favorite abstract artists, Gerhard Richter, also born in 1932, whose many paintings are appreciated for their sun-drenched tonalities."

Haiku Song 1932

Doves fly out
of a beggar's coffee can—
leaving behind a few dimes.

Inspired by the song "Brother, Can You Spare Me A Dime?" Composed by wordsmith Yip Harburg and music by Jay Gorney for the Broadway show *Americana*. One scene featured a breadline where a man is no longer recognized by his friends ("Say, don't you remember? I'm your pal"). "Brother, Can You Spare Me a Dime?" became a powerful and poignant topical song. Harburg's lyrics are so well written each verse digs deeper and deeper into the human heart, serving as America's Great Depression Anthem song. Versions by both Bing Crosby on Brunswick Records and Rudy Vallée on Columbia were hit songs.
    "Yip, yip hurrah!" Later, lyricist Yip Harburg would provide the lyrics for the 1939 song "Over the Rainbow," with music by Harold Arlen, which would become their signature if not masterpiece song.

Haiku Instrumental 1933
A Stormy Weather Nursery Rhyme

Seek tethers in stormy weather,
if it's my hand . . .
we'll stay together.

Inspired by "Stormy Weather" by legendary Harold Arlen and co-writer Ted Koehler, and performed by Duke Ellington's Orchestra. Even though the song was composed by two "white guys," "Stormy Weather" would have a strong influence on the African American plight in American cinema.

Haiku Song 1933
To Dream In Purple Heather

We read Bronte—
dream in purple heather,
forgetting stormy weather.

Inspired by the song version of "Stormy Weather," composed by lyricist Ted Koehler and music by the great Harold Arlen (who in 1939 will achieve mythical standards with "Over The Rainbow"). "Stormy Weather" was first sung by Arlen himself, who rarely recorded, but Koehler and Arlen felt the song should be given to a female vocalist, and so in came Ethel Waters of the Cotton Club and brought down the house in May of 1933! The song would become legendary and more so 10 years later when Lena Horne sings "Stormy Weather" in the film of the same title. Then Judy Garland would have a go at it with resounding success in 1961.

Haiku Instrumental 1934

She said, "the world has gone up-side-down!"
I check for keys
and for loose change.

Inspired by "Stomping At The Savoy" by Harlem's finest, Chick Webb, and co-authored with Benny Goodman and arranger Edgar Sampson. Chick Webb's Savoy Orchestra recorded this jitterbug dance classic in May of 1934. It is one of the finest dance-tunes ever co-authored by both a black and white American: Webb and Goodman. The "King of Swing" Big Band leader Benny Goodman (a white Chicagoan) often immersed himself in black music, and worked and performed with black musicians—a touch of civil grace in the mid-thirties, yet we still have some ways to go.

Haiku Song 1934

Sign swings at an
abandoned gas station,
a tumbleweed rolls on by.

Inspired by "Tumbling Tumbleweeds," composed by Bob Nolan for the Country Music vocal group Sons of The Pioneers, featuring the wonderful Roy Rogers, later followed by a bigger hit from the singing cowboy-hero Gene Autry in 1935. Gene Autry helped jumpstart the Country-Western music industry and the genre of singing western movies. As a child I loved Gene Autry and his movies. I grew up next door to a family of 14 children and on Saturday mornings we'd sit in front of the TV with neighborhood kids and watch him heroically sing and ride into the sunset. After every Autry movie the boys would ask me to sing his trademark song, "Back In The Saddle Again," as my buddies Armaan, Herrera, Eddie, Steady-Teddy, Ozzie, Andy, Bony Tony, Vick-the-Stick, Curtis, Joe-Bow, and Joe would howl like coyotes!

Haiku Instrumental 1935

I'm drawn to eternity,
but I'll be happy
if you stay awhile.

Inspired by *Romeo And Juliet Suite* by Sergei Prokofiev. This suite is powerful and rapturous at times. What I find attractive about it is seeing Shakespeare's play set to a ballet. But with an even closer listen you can hear a prelude of traumatic melodies, as if Prokofiev was saying to his audience, "fellow Russians, prepare yourselves, we are about to go to war with Germany."

Haiku Song 1935

When winter's at zero sublime
may I take you in
like summertime.

Inspired by "Summertime," music by George Gershwin and lyrics by Du Bose Heyward and Ira Gershwin from the opera *Porgy and Bess*. The two Gershwin brothers loved a book simply entitled *Porgy*, which contained a series of Southern vignettes by South Carolinian author Du Bose Heyward. They asked Heyward to create the libretto, while Ira contributed to a few of the songs. The opera ran with its share of controversy, as many felt the Southern stereotyping was a bit harsh on the African American's plight, yet at least 10 songs became classic tunes, particularly following the 1959 motion-picture musical starring Sidney Poitier. Some of my favorite recordings are
    "Bess, You Is My Woman Now" sung by Robert McFerrin and Adele Addison, 1959
    "I Loves You, Porgy" sung by Nina Simone, 1959 and The Bill Evans Trio performing it as an instrumental at the Village Vanguard, 1961;
    "Summertime" sung by Billie Holiday in 1936 and Ella Fitzgerald and Louis Armstrong in 1957; and Janis Joplin with the Big Brother and the Holding Company in 1968.

Haiku Instrumental 1936

"Hey, the music stopped."
"Has Earth stopped too?"
"No."
"Good, then why don't we dance!"

Inspired by "Echoes of Harlem" by Duke Ellington and His Orchestra featuring Cootie Williams on trumpet. It's hard to imagine that as the country was struggling to get out of the Great Depression, music in Harlem was at its richest! Just about every night an orchestra was hopping and young folks were dancing . . . call it a release from reality.

Haiku Song 1936
At The Crossroads

At the crossroads,
with hellhounds on my trail . . .
I must run or go to jail.

I reach for a coin:
if it flips tails, I sail—
if heads, I seek my bail.

Inspired by two songs by Robert Johnson: "Crossroad Blues" and "Hellhounds On My Trail." Johnson was a music "visionary immortal." He was discovered in 1936 and his flame burned for a mere two years. Like a comet he recorded 29 original tracks, plus an amazing 13 original alternates for Columbia Records. By August of 1938 he was gone forever. Johnson opened the floodgates for other Blues and folk singers to write their own songs instead of seeking out professional songwriters. For example, thanks to Johnson, Woody Guthrie, Hank Williams, and Chuck Berry became songsmith legends. Johnson was also a great guitar player with a style uniquely his own that later became a benchmark for guitarists like Charlie Christian, Joe Pass, Wes Montgomery, Grant Green, Les Paul, Scotty Moore, Carl Perkins, Eric Clapton, Jimmy Page, Pete Townsend, Jeff Beck, Duane Allman, and Jimi Hendrix.

    Robert Johnson is one of the reasons this book of music haikus was created. No Robert Johnson, no book. . . that simple.

Haiku Instrumental 1937
On the Brink of War

As the pendulum swings
we wait in between;
pins will fall, as foreseen.

Inspired by "Sing, Sing, Sing (With A Swing)" performed by Benny Goodman and His Orchestra. Like Louis Armstrong's "Potato Head Blues," this is a groundbreaking piece. I also like to compare "Sing, Sing, Sing" to Stravinsky's *Rite of Spring*—both monumental in presentation and overwhelming in expression! True, Stravinsky single-handedly caused a riot with his work, but Benny Goodman open-handedly caused all people of all ages and ethnicities to DANCE! The composer and performers of "Sing, Sing, Sing" were all of different ethnic backgrounds: Louis Prima (composer), an Italian American; Gene Krupa (the great drum pioneer), of Polish decent from Chicago; and Benny Goodman, an American Russian Jew who often employed and played with Black Americans. It was a melting pot of delicious American stew. Composed just two years before WWII broke out in Europe, the piece, which runs around nine minutes, is hopeful, rambunctious, primitive and most importantly—IT SWINGS!

Haiku Song 1937

Valentine names are faded
and slightly dated,
yet . . . how I waited.

Inspired by "My Funny Valentine," composed by Lorenz Hart (words) and Richard Rodgers (music), aka Rodgers and Hart. The song was first sung by Mitzi Green in the 1937 Broadway musical *Babes In Arms*. It seemed charming enough but didn't quite get off the ground. Judy Garland also sang it in *Babes In Arms* (the motion picture) and it too seemed enjoyable yet not significant. Jump to the mid-1950s as featured in the musical *Pal Joey* and it became a sensation. It also became a Jazz standard after the young and cool trumpeter Miles Davis played it so soulfully in his classic 1956 album *Cookin' With The Miles Davis Quintet*.

Like the song "As Time Goes By," "My Funny Valentine" is an American institution. Since the 1950s it has become one of the top 10 most recorded songs. On October 15, 1992 I played "My Funny Valentine" on piano for my wife Cristina in a nightclub on Ikebukuro Street in Tokyo, Japan.

Haiku Instrumental 1938
of things ancient and new

"Grandma,
why do I go to school?"
"To help you
utilize life's tools."

"Grandma,
what good is sleeping?"
"It's when you
take the time for dreaming."

"Grandma,
why swim to the other side?"
"To know that deep rivers
run wide."

"Grandma,
why are some months so cold?"
"Because there's loved ones
we need to hold."

"Grandma,
why are we here?"
"To know someone who'll love you
will always be near."

Haiku inspired by *Adagio For Strings, op.11* by Samuel Barber. It is difficult to believe this piece of music was composed in 1936 (and re-scored in 1938). Barber's most well-known work feels as ancient as the beginning of time, yet modern as today. For many people, the composition is deeply personal and has often appeared in plays, stories, and most of all motion pictures. Yet, with so much exposure over the years, anyone would think *Adagio For Strings* has worn out its welcome, but it has proven stronger than ever as it approaches its 100th year, proving its enduring timelessness.

Haiku Song 1938

Tired from dancing all night
we fall asleep
before saying "goodnight."

Inspired by "Two Sleepy People" composed by Hoagy Carmichael and Frank Loesser. In mid-1938 the motion picture *Thanks For The Memory*, starring Bob Hope and Shirley Ross, introduced "Two Sleepy People," but it didn't move much until later that year when the vibrant composer, entertainer, and National Treasure Fats Waller made it a sensation in November of that year.

Haiku Instrumental 1939

Deep in soul searching,
I pause
to bite a chocolate-dipped pretzel . . . oh . . . OH!

Inspired by the instrumental version of "Body And Soul" as performed by Colman Hawkins. Coleman Hawkins' instrumental version was recorded in October of 1939 and became quite the marvel. Many felt it was miraculous that Hawkins, a Black Jazz musician, had been able to cross over to the Pop chart ratings, but I argue differently. The song and Colman Hawkins' version is an inescapable masterpiece that could not be contained! (Note that "Body And Soul" appears in "Haiku Song 1930.")

Haiku Song 1939
Two Masterpieces

(Haiku Inspired by "Strange Fruit"):

"Grandma, what's a strange fruit?"
"It hangs on a tree
you never forget."

(Haiku Inspired by "Over The Rainbow"):

Astronaut takes photos,
hums "Over The Rainbow"—
a tear floats by Earth.

Two haikus inspired by two songs from two very different neighborhoods that simply cannot be ignored. Both songs reach a deep fundamental cord which touches our humanity so that we may NEVER FORGET and NEVER STOP DREAMING!

In early 1939 schoolteacher Lewis Allen (real name Abel Meeropol) presented "Strange Fruit" to a deeply moved Billie Holiday. The moment she heard it she realized her life was going to change if she recorded the song. By using lynching as a bleak metaphor, it exposed American racism to its core. Both melody and lyrics weave a piece of music which holds you through every stunning note. Billie Holiday initially went to her Columbia label, but they refused to record it. So she went to the smaller label Commodore Records and recorded "Strange Fruit" on April 20, 1939, becoming Billie Holiday's best-selling song.

"Over The Rainbow" was composed by Harold Arlen (music) and E.Y. Harburg (lyrics) for Judy Garland to sing in the motion picture *The Wizard of Oz*. What's amazing is that the song was almost deleted from the film, if it hadn't been for Arthur Freed, the producer, insisting it remain. "Over The Rainbow" became Judy Garland's theme song and world-wide hit. Since 1939 innumerable articles, books, music thesis, and history references have been devoted to this three-minute award winning song.

Haiku Instrumental 1940

"Ummm, I'm in the mood."
"I'm so dense! You know the game's tied . . .
let's watch TV!"

Inspired by "In The Mood" as performed by Glenn Miller and His Orchestra, composed by Joe Garland, Wingy Manone and Andy Razaf. 1939 was the breakout year for Miller and his Big Band, and he would become a legend both for his music and his wartime service. In 1942, at the peak of the Big Band era, Miller gave up a lucrative civilian career and joined the war effort, serving in the Army Air Forces where he eventually formed a traveling wartime band. However, on December 15, 1944 his airplane disappeared over the English Channel. To this day no one knows exactly the circumstances of his disappearance. The following year, his wife Helen Miller accepted the Bronze Star medal for Miller.

Haiku Song 1940

I didn't have a clue
until I knew
and missed the nearness of you.

Inspired by "The Nearness of You," composed by Hoagy Carmichael (music) and Ned Washington (lyrics), and performed by Glenn Miller and His Orchestra, featuring Ray Eberle on vocals. "The Nearness of You" is a perfect example of a romantic love song without being overly sentimental, thanks to the genius of Big Band leader Glenn Miller. Over the years, Carmichael's "The Nearness of You" has led me to some great *"near you"* love songs, such as:

Kay Starr, "Side By Side" (1953)
Ben E. King, "Stand By Me" (1961)
The Beatles, "Norwegian Wood (This Bird Has Flown)" (1965)
The Beach Boys, "Don't Talk (Put Your Head On My Shoulder)" (1966)
The Carpenters, "(They Long To Be) Close To You" (1970)
Roberta Flack and Donny Hathaway, "The Closer I Get To You" (1978)
Sade, "By Your Side" (2000)

Haiku Instrumental 1941

From Manhattan
to Brooklyn
the "A" passes through like a rolling pin.

Inspired by "Take The 'A' Train" by Duke Ellington and His Orchestra. The word "united" in United States of America came to fruition with the sound of railroad tracks being laid on America's soil, and the sound of "Take The 'A' Train" is, to my mind, an archetype of this unity. This magical program-piece mimics the sound of the famous New York City subway route with layers of moving horns and the click-clack of the beat. It makes you snap your fingers and shuffle your feet choo-choo style! It quickly became Duke's signature piece, due in part to his great pre-war orchestra musicians, three of whom were Ben Webster on tenor sax, Johnny Hodges on alto sax, and Ray Nance taking on two trumpet solos.

"Take The 'A' Train" is one of many great works authored by the remarkable Billy Strayhorn. Both Ellington and Strayhorn worked closely together up until Billy's death in 1967. Billy, a true American hero, was both a proud black man and openly gay during an era when both characteristics would have brought him great suffering. But Ellington admired Billy as one of America's most important musical icons of the 20th century. American heroes both!

Haiku Song 1941

"So this is your solar-system mobile . . .
which planet is your favorite?"
". . . Earth."

Inspired by "Where In The World," composed by Ray Austin, Paul Herrick and Freddy Martin, and sung by singer-actor Tony Martin. Recorded in May of 1941 and issued in 1942, I find that this hauntingly beautiful song is like an echo of Beethoven's adagio from his *7th Symphony*. It would be ear-opening to listen to both pieces, first the 7 minute adagio then "Where In the World," an example of the continuity and unity of music through time.

Haiku Instrumental 1942

Soldier with his ration can of peas
hears "String of Pearls"
on radio.

Inspired by "String of Pearls" by Glenn Miller and His Orchestra. Composed and arranged by Jerry Gray on Bluebird Records. "String of Pearls" was a colossal hit for Miller at a time when WWII was looming on the horizon for Americans.

    Glenn Miller would soon enlist and members of his orchestra served as both fighting soldiers and performers for the troops. As mentioned earlier, he disappeared in 1944 when his plane was lost over the English Channel.

Haiku Song 1942
. . . *of Christmas And Hope*

Your warm wood stove,
the silence of snow,
now there's nowhere I need to go.

Inspired by "White Christmas," words and music by Irving Berlin. Treatises have been written about this masterpiece, and for good reason. Both words and music weave perfectly together to create an experience of joy during the Holiday Season and the archetypal connection to wintertime. In October of 1942 the motion picture *Holiday Inn* featured Bing Crosby performing the song. America had been deep at war now for eleven months and "White Christmas" was welcomed as a gift of hope by the American soldiers and Allies in Europe and Asia. Much like Harold Arlen's "Over The Rainbow," to dream was to keep faith in humanity! With "Over The Rainbow" we dreamed to go beyond borders, and with "White Christmas" we dreamed to make it back home.

Haiku Instrumental 1943
Letter From Home

"Dear Papa,
I've placed a wooden soldier
in my dollhouse . . .
hurry back."

Inspired by "Letter From Home" (1943-44) by Aaron Copland. America's National Classical composer was born in 1900, the same year Rachmaninov composed his *Piano Concerto no. 2*; the Romantic overtones of that piece must have crept into the newborn's ear that year. Copland lived until 1990 and managed to walk on the fringe between Late Romanticism and Modernism unscathed. Copland was very prolific in the 1940s with ballets, film scores, and orchestral works. Between 1943-1944 he composed one of his greatest works, *Appalachian Spring*, while finding time to compose "Letter From Home."

Haiku Song 1943
Homage To Spitfire

. . . made paper doll angels
till one caught fire with embers afloat . . .
"Look, wings."

Inspired by the song "Paper Doll," as performed by the Mills Brothers. The song was first composed in the early 1930s by Johnny S. Black. In 1943 it resurfaced in the motion picture *Hi Good Lookin'* and "Paper Doll" became the biggest non-holiday hit of the decade. The Homage to Spitfire is in reference to the most important WWII British crafted plane, relentlessly serving the Royal Air Force, the Royal Canadian Air Force, the United States Army Air Force, plus 29 more military Alliances.

Haiku Instrumental 1944

At Appalachian sunrise
my blank easel and I
will compromise.

Inspired by *Appalachian Spring* by Aaron Copland. America has been blessed with many great painters who have depicted the American landscape with depth, beauty and awe. Music too depicts the American landscape and Copland's *Appalachian Spring* powerfully encapsulates this American spirit. It was a ballet composed for legendary Martha Graham right-smack during WWII. In spite of all the global suffering, Copland managed to create a piece of great beauty. *Appalachian Spring* can be heard on CD in two formats: either as a suite, or the ballet in its entirety (which runs about 40 minutes). Either version is amazing!

Haiku Song 1944

Her face on a soldier's tattoo—
Christmas card reads
"I'll be seeing you."

Inspired by both "Have Yourself A Merry Little Christmas" and "I'll Be Seeing You."

    "Have Yourself A Merry Little Christmas" was composed by Ralph Blane (words) and Hugh Martin (music) for the motion picture *Meet Me In St. Louis*. It became a Holiday masterpiece and ranks in the top eight of the most covered Holiday Season songs of all times; and after "Over The Rainbow," became Judy Garland's second theme-song.

    "I'll Be Seeing You" was composed by Irving Kahal (words) and Sammy Fain (music) for the 1938 musical *Right This Way*. The song went virtually unnoticed until in 1944 it became one of the greatest ballads of WWII. Many artists recorded the classic song during the WWII years, such as Bing Crosby, Connee Boswell, Billie Holiday, and Tommy Dorsey (featuring Frank Sinatra).

Haiku Instrumental 1945

Sometimes there's
plenty of room for 'anyhow'
then there's 'the time is now.'

Inspired by the instrumental "Now's The Time" by Charlie "Bird" Parker. The legendary alto sax player was born in Kansas City in 1920 but spent his years in New York City. Many of the musicians joining 'Bird' on the November 26, 1945 recording session of "Now's The Time" would become Jazz legends: Dizzy Gillespie, Curly Russell, Max Roach, and a young Miles Davis.

Haiku Song 1945
A Study On Guthrie's
"This Land Is Your Land"

This highway looks like a ribbon
on a present
I long to open.

This skyway looks like an endless kite
on a tail-line
I long to chase.

This land looks like a painting
resting on an easel
for all to share.

Inspired by "This Land Is Your Land," words and music by Woody Guthrie, composed in 1940 but not published until 1945. By then America had gone through Prohibition, the Great Depression, and two world wars, yet every decade there was something new in music to enjoy.

    In the 20th century we would witness extraordinary pioneers create or alter music, such as Louis Armstrong, Duke Ellington, and Robert Johnson. Woody Guthrie was one of those pioneers, the most important American folk music artist of the first-half of the 20th century. Born dirt-poor in 1912 Oklahoma, he was amongst those who experienced the Great Dustbowl diaspora.

    A troubadour in the truest sense, Guthrie's wanderlust led him to create songs of the land, protest songs, union songs, country songs, anti-war songs, environmental songs, and children's songs. In his short life Woody set the stage for songs of American roots music to the highest standard. Every folk musician and songwriter soon learned to follow suit.

Haiku Instrumental 1946

"Grandma, what are
Roman amphitheaters?"
". . . First, get the breadbasket."

Inspired by "A Night In Tunisia" by Dizzy Gillespie. The composition was composed by Gillespie and Frank Paparelli in 1942, yet my favorite version is his Victor Records recording from February 22, 1946. This piece is easily one of the top most covered Jazz tunes of the 20th century.

    I have loved "A Night In Tunisia" since childhood and its middle-eastern style led me to discover Hamza El Din's classic 1964 album *Music of Nubia*, leading me to a life-long love affair with the classical styles of Middle Eastern music. Funny how Dizzy, an East Coast guy with a trumpet and a beatnik beret, would show me the way to the Middle East.

Haiku Song 1946

When good times roll
I kiss barber-poles, hot coals,
trolls and highway patrols.

(. . . Hey, I'm on a Roll!)

Teach me how to bowl—
dance out-of-control
and wiggle out my soul.

Inspired by the song "Let The Good Times Roll," composed by Sam Theard and Fleecie Moore, as sung by early Rhythm and Blues (R&B) artist Louis Jordan on Decca Records. This joyful, danceable and expressive song easily served as a symbol of relief for a decade that had seen much suffering. By the mid 1940s R&B kick-started into high speed and would grow into the 1950s to meld into something no one anticipated: Rock 'n' Roll!

Haiku Instrumental 1947

At the gate-of-sleep
I give a slight chuckle
just before falling deep.

Inspired by "'Round Midnight" by Jazz genius Thelonious Monk. It was believed he composed this masterpiece as early as 1940-41. He bopped around with it in New York City until he finally got to lay-it-down in late 1947 for Blue Note Records. "'Round Midnight" instantly became a classic.

    As a young boy, the first time I heard "'Round Midnight" was not by Monk but rather Miles Davis' 1957 recording of it. Miles' version is believed to be one of the greatest Jazz classics of all time, especially when John Coltrane blows his solo through the night air of 'midnight.' Later, lyrics were added, and if you ever wish to be thrilled with its moody words, please listen to Mel Tormé's version . . . it is nocturnally blissful!

Haiku Song 1947

Before ripping dry-wall
we found his map
of the Wabash Cannonball.

Inspired by "Wabash Cannonball," first credited to A.J. Roff in 1882, then undergoing many changes throughout the years until it ended up in the hands of the Carter Family who issued it in 1932. Country-Western artist Roy Acuff recorded two versions of the song, one in 1938 and a live version in 1947. Both were smash hits.

When I was a child, my aunt Lycha had a model train-set that included houses and building structures. I would walk for many blocks from home to see her and play with that train-set, absorbed for hours in my own make-believe-world. Whenever I hear "Wabash Cannonball" it sends me right back to my imaginary world of trains.

One of the most famous stretches of the Wabash Cannonball Line runs through upper Ohio. The line and tracks started to die off from 1971 to 1992, and for years remained a ghostly unkempt stretch. Then in the mid-1990s all counties in the upper Ohio region raised money to create the Wabash Cannonball Trail, a 63 mile multi-use recreational trail in Northwest Ohio. It's a trail for all ages and activities, from simple hikes to competitive sport events to camping along the once legendary line. I guess the imagination of a train lingers longer than we might expect.

Haiku Instrumental 1948

Playful pony
dewdrop prancing—
I cut an apple
it stops dancing.

Inspired by *The Red Pony Suite* by Aaron Copland, composed as Incidental music for the 1949 motion picture *The Red Pony* directed by Lewis Milestone and starring Myrna Loy, Robert Mitchum, and Peter Miles. The film was based on John Steinbeck's classic short story of a boy's love for a red pony. A 1973 television film version starred Henry Ford and Maureen O'Hara.

Haiku Song 1948
There was a boy . . .

Boy rings prayer bowl
at his feet:
love,
joy,
life,
death,
rebirth,
all complete.

Inspired by "Nature Boy," composed by Eden Ahbez, a wandering Yogi-nomad who often lived under Los Angeles freeway ramps and under the famous "Hollywood" sign. Nat "King" Cole acquired the sheet music and absolutely loved the soulfully-hypnotic composition. He recorded the song with Capitol Records in 1947, just before the American Federation of Musicians Royalty strike. Released in 1948, "Nature Boy" became a huge hit. Of interest is that the first few measure of the melody have elements of Antonín Dvořák's "Dumka, Andante" from his 1887 *Piano Quintet in A Major*, which just goes to show that greatness is not born in a vacuum.

   I have loved this song since I turned 12, partly due to my grandmother. Every Friday I was responsible for accompanying her to our local Kmart store, which had a deli of things she enjoyed. The walk was just over a mile and this became our ritual for years. She would wait for me to get home from school and off we'd go. I was an obstinate young teen, at first resentful that I had to take this walk with my grandmother, but soon our hearts pumped and conversation flew. Then, without fail, at the corner of Iris Street and South Ventura Road, she'd gently sing to me Nat "King" Cole's "Nature Boy" in Spanish. Decades have now passed, yet every time I hear "Nature Boy" I try to catch strains of my grandmother's elusive voice.

Haiku Instrumental 1949

You left me on Foggy Top
with torn wedding vows
and a *milkless* cow.

Inspired by "Foggy Mountain Breakdown" by Lester Flatt and Earl Scruggs with The Foggy Mountain Boys. Composed by Scruggs in 1949 and recorded that December. With this joyful and lightning-fast tune, Scruggs lived up to be the world's greatest banjoist! And Flatt was one of the world's greatest guitarists. Countless articles have been written regarding this Bluegrass masterpiece, and I will throw in my two cents to say that if you need just one example to explain Bluegrass music, play this up-beat 'breakdown' and just listen . . . you will understand what makes Bluegrass uniquely American.

Haiku Song 1949

I'm so lonesome and homesick
my weeping tears
drown out the candle wick.

Inspired by "I'm So Lonesome I Could Cry," composed and performed by Hank Williams. What makes Hank Williams stand out as a 20th century pioneer is that while most Country music singers outsourced "catchy-tunes" from other composers and songsmiths, Hank came straight out of nowhere authoring most of his own material. Williams, being dirt poor like Woody Guthrie, pushed himself hard to create his own songs because he had little money to buy cover songs from others. Hank's influence has affected just about every folk artist, country artist, root music artist, folk rock artist, and even left droplets in R&B (see Ray Charles)—remarkable achievement for a person to shine so brightly so briefly. Like Robert Johnson, Hank Williams' brightness couldn't stop his deep self-destructiveness. Hank would be gone at 29 years of age.
    Other Hank Williams songs I enjoy are:

"Move It On Over"
"Your Cheatin' Heart"
"(Your) Cold, Cold Heart"
"Jambalaya"
"I Saw The Light"
 "My Son Calls Another Man Daddy"
"I Can't Help It (If I'm still in love with you)"
"Hey Good Lookin'"
 "Honky Tonk Blues"
 "Alone And Forsaken"
"I'll Never Get Out of This World Alive"

Haiku Instrumental 1950

Don't send money—
blow kisses in the air . . .
I'll await delivery.

Inspired by "Moon Dreams" by The Miles Davis Nonet (featuring conductor Gil Evans) from the classic Jazz album *The Birth of Cool*. "Moon Dreams," composed by Chummy MacGregor and Johnny Mercer, was first recorded in 1942 by Glen Miller, then re-released by Miles Davis in 1950. *"Cool"* was in the air, in our poetry, literature, American and European films, and in Jazz thanks to Miles.

Haiku Song 1950

When the world was young
I found old things.
I'm older now, in a young world.

Inspired by "When The World Was Young," originally a French song by composer M. Philippe-Gerard. In 1950 English words were added by the great lyricist Johnny Mercer, who would go on to create a masterpiece, "Moon River," with Henry Mancini in 1961. "When The World Was Young" was covered by many artists in the 1950s but my favorite is Peggy Lee's 1956 version.

Haiku Instrumental 1951
A Child's Lullaby

"Stardust, save me
from bad weather—
I'm fine if you're just pillow feathers."

Inspired by "Stardust," composed by Hoagy Carmichael back in 1927 but performed here on December 26, 1951 by Ben Webster. Webster was one of three "Swing Jazz" tenor sax giants along with Colman Hawkins and Lester Young, yet no one came close to Webster's ballads, a gentle giant pouring out arias into the air. Magical! (Also see the 1931 version in this book.)

Haiku Song 1951

Roller-skates, soapbox,
teddy-bear driver roll bar . . .
my very first car!

Inspired by "Rocket 88" by Jackie Brenston and His Delta Cats, penned by R&B saxophonist Brenston. In March of 1951 legendary record producer Sam Phillips recorded Brenston and his song in Memphis, Tennessee for Chess Records, taking "Rocket 88" to the R&B moon! Plus, many music historians consider "Rocket 88' to be a prelude to the dawn of Rock 'n' Roll.

    I was 8 when I first heard this song and thought it was performed by jumpin' Martians. . . simply out-of-this-world! Revolutionary! When my next birthday came around I asked for lumber so I could build my first Go-cart, and with my enamel car model paints I christened my Go-cart "Rocket 88." It was my first car!

Haiku Instrumental 1952

"Choo, choo—
my hand loves your railroad spine . . ."
"What journey do you hope to find?"

Inspired by "Night Train" by Jimmy Forrest. In the mid-1940s R&B was born. In March of 1952 Jimmy Forrest's "Night Train" became a huge hit and it would again become famous in 1962 with James Brown's vocal version *funking*-it-up!

Haiku Song 1952

(Extrovert version)
When you're gone I sleep like a cat—
when you're home, I'm a crazy hound dog.

(Introvert version)
When you're gone I'm a crazy hound dog—
when you're home, I'm a tame cat.

Inspired by "Hound Dog." LADIES AND GENTS, "BIG MAMA" THORNTON IS IN THE HOUSE! In 1952 composers Jerry Leiber and Mike Stoller were looking for someone to sing their R&B song "Hound Dog." In August of 1952, the two *white boys* got their wish! "Hound Dog," much like "Rocket 88," has early hints of Rock 'n' Roll weaving its magic web.

    This was Big Mama's territory, and Leiber and Stoller knew the three of them would make history, and they were right as the world listened, including a young man from Tupelo, Mississippi. . .Elvis!

Haiku Instrumental 1953

I used to hunt
for rarest rubies
now I see them in raspberries.

Inspired by "'Ruby," music by Heinz Roemheld as performed by Richard Hayman and His Orchestra. Hayman was a Hollywood music artist wearing many hats: phenomenal harmonica player, arranger, composer and bandleader. One of his first jobs was as an "unaccredited" music arranger in the film *Meet Me In St. Louis* (as I mentioned before, one of my all-time favorite movies). The first time I heard the lyric version of "Ruby" was by Ray Charles in 1960 who sang "Ruby" with great exhilaration! Oh, and let's not forget Thelonious Monk's version for solo piano.

Haiku Song 1953
From Paradise

I felt less a man
lost in Paradise Land
till you said, "take my hand."

Inspired by "Stranger In Paradise," composed for the 1953 musical *Kismet* with music adapted from Russian Romantic composer Alexander Borodin, who died back in 1887. Tin Pan Alley songwriters often went to the Classics to create popular songs, and this concept continues today! The two lyricists Robert Wright and George Forrest completed "Stranger In Paradise" using the melody of Borodin's "Polovtsian Dances" from his opera *Prince Igor*.

Touched by the Divine

I was a boy when I first fell in love with Tony Bennett's honeyed voice singing "Stranger In Paradise" through our church speakers, coming to us like an act of divine intervention. From that point on I thought Bennett was the voice of God and for decades I dared not utter his name in vain! In my room I worshiped every single record album of "He that remained name-less"... I know this sounds crazy but hey, I have issues.

Jump forward a few decades, my wife and I had tickets to see Tony Bennett at the Sonoma Wine Festival. As we waited for him to come on stage she said to me, "Dave, we've been together for a couple of decades and not once have I heard you say *TONY BENNETT*. You either say, his *Eminence, Divine One, He That Remains Name-less*, or nothing at all ... don't you think it's kinda strange?" I responded by telling her my church story, but she stopped me and replied, "I know that story. Yes, so you had been *touched by the divine*, so what will happen if you find yourself on your last breath and you refuse to utter the true name of The One That Remains Name-less ... who are you cheating then?" So I made a promise to her that the moment *he* walked on stage I would shout out his NAME!

There we were waiting in the audience and I was so nervous to see him walk on stage that I got the skiddies and had to run for the restroom, and so missed his grand entrance and his first two songs. However, I made it back just as he started his third song with "Rags To Riches" and along with the euphoric audience I shouted "VIVA, TONY BENNETT! VIVA TONY BENNETT!"

Haiku Instrumental 1954

"What must I do? You head into mist
just as we've kissed."
"Persist, persist . . ."

Inspired by "Misty" by Erroll Garner, an instrumental that also entered the Pop charts in October of 1954 and ushered in a misty autumn mood. I highly suggest two lyric versions of "Misty" which many of you may already know: Ella Fitzgerald's 1960 version with just her angelic voice and one piano; and Johnny Mathis' 1959 version, his trademark song and one of the most popular versions ever.

Haiku Song 1954

You can take me to the moon
or disco
but my heart stays in *Frisco*!

Inspired by "Fly Me To The Moon (or, In Other Words)" and "I Left My Heart In San Francisco." Both songs have similar journeys, yes journeys. Both were first published in 1954 but faded until their rebirth in 1962. "Fly Me To The Moon (or, In other words)" was composed by Bart Howard in 1954 but flew nowhere (no pun intended). However, by 1962 the NASA Space Program was creating enormous public interest and "Fly Me To The Moon" had its rebirth! Between 1962 to 1964 over fifty performers recorded it and was hugely popular with Jazz artists following the West Coast Jazz Sound and the Bossa Nova Jazz craze.

"I Left My Heart In San Francisco" composed by Douglass A. Cross and George Cory in 1953-54 immediately faded from view. But in 1962, during a mega-music shift into a Rock 'n' Roll world, Tony Bennett found himself a place of refuge singing standards at the San Francisco Fairmont Hotel. Cross and Cory reworked their song for Bennett, transforming him into an icon in a new *Pop* world. "I Left My Heart In San Francisco" received many music awards and clearly became Bennett's theme song. Tony has been singing this song for over 60 years and wherever he is performing it there is an audience going crazy!

Haiku Instrumental 1955
A Child's First Letter to Earth

"Hot Sun above the North Pole,
please be patient with us—
start with my trust."

Inspired by *The Goldberg Variations* by Johann Sebastian Bach, as performed and recorded by pianist Glenn Gould in 1955. The *Variations* was first published in 1742 for harpsichord and consisted of an aria with 30 variations. By 1955 this piece was seldom performed and rarely recorded. Canadian Classical pianist Glenn Gould took the challenge in the early 1950s and worked on the *Variations* for almost two years (not for harpsichord but for piano). In 1955 it paid off! The recording turned Gould into a superstar and Columbia a major contender in the Classical market. By early 1956 the sales were beyond belief for a Classical album. It was reported to have sold 40,000 copies by 1960 and had sold more than 100,000 by the time of Gould's death in 1982.

The Price And The Last Payoff

Glenn Gould would go on to perform and record albums (another one of my Gould favorites is the 1963 Bach's *Toccatas and Inventions*) but fame came with a price. Gould was well known for various eccentricities—from his eccentric Classical analyses to unpredictable body movements with humming and vocal sounds while at the keyboard. In 1964, at the age of 31, he stopped performing concerts to concentrate on studio recordings and other projects. Gould would disappear from time to time, and then show up walking around New York City (always in heavy winter attire, even in summer) or popping into Columbia Studios to work his genius for the label. In 1981 he would show up at Columbia Studios and rewrite music history (see Haiku Instrumental 1981).

Haiku Song 1955

"Nine, ten, eleven O'clock—
where's your socks,
don't call your doc . . .
let's go rock!"

"Twelve, one, two O'clock rock—
Happy New Year!"
"Yeah, but we never left here!"

Inspired by "(We're Gonna) Rock Around The Clock," composed by Max Freedman and Jimmy DeKnight, as performed by Bill Haley and the Comets. This is not the first Rock 'n' Roll song, but it is the first one to go mainstream. Haley's song created the "sound wall" that distinguished the Rock Era from the Pop tunes that came before. Haley at first was a Country Swing bandleader till he caught the Rock 'n' Roll bug. Though first composed in 1954, it shot to prominence when it became the theme song in the 1955 motion picture *The Blackboard Jungle* starring Glenn Ford. Young people lined up in droves to see the film and in some movie theatres riots broke out as the song played. Rock 'n' Roll had arrived!

Haiku Instrumental 1956
...of Things Enchanted

I'm still drawn to heart-felt thunder
and things which bring
euphoric wonder.

Inspired by "Diminuendo In Blue And Crescendo In Blue" by Duke Ellington and His Orchestra, performed live at the Newport Jazz Festival on July 7, 1956. On this enchanted evening the group opened the program with a suite composed by Ellington specifically for the Festival. He wanted to create something new and hip as his popularity had been waning, and the advent of the Bebop and Cool Jazz culture was shadowing over his shoulders. The reception of Ellington's *Newport Suite* was polite but lukewarm. Duke had wished for a larger impact, so he pulled out both "Diminuendo In Blue" and "Crescendo In Blue" from his 1938 catalogue and asked tenor saxophonist Paul Gonsalves to join the two works in a full swing interval the likes of which had never been heard before. As Gonsalves began to "dig in," a platinum blonde Marilyn Monroe-look-a-like in a black dress jumped out of her box seat, rushed to the front of the stage, and began dancing in a joyous frenzy! Duke took this opportunity to goad Gonsalves even further, and thus what followed were 27 choruses of euphoric swing!
    Pandemonium at Newport broke out as the crowd began cheering, rushing the stage, and dancing. Many audience members stood on their chairs leading a crazy dance. Gonsalves was creating music history, for as the show was being aired live the entire East Coast almost stopped in mid-traffic. Hysteria was ablaze! The Newport Festival management rushed the side-stage and asked Ellington to cool the tempo down as the crowd showed no sign of letting up. So Ellington broke into a blues-ballad, "Jeep's Blues," performed by the great alto saxophonist Johnny Hodges, but this made the audience just as excited. After a few more songs the audience did calm down before the Newport recording left us with an eternal gift to reflect on!

I first heard "Diminuendo In Blue And Crescendo In Blue" during a middle-grade school music class. School being difficult for me at the time, the teacher placed me in the back row to simply listen but not participate. As "Diminuendo In Blue And Crescendo In Blue" played I sat in amazement and just as the piece ended at nearly 15-minutes of cosmic wonder, I quietly left the classroom, walked out to the hall and cried tears of joy because I had been born into a new era of musical awakening.

(This book would not have existed if not for this euphoric wonder!)

Haiku Song 1956

Throwing unread Valentines
in a dust bin,
I sing "Heartbreak Hotel."

Inspired by "Heartbreak Hotel," composed by Mae Boren Axton, Tommy Durden, and Elvis Presley. This was the first RCA Record hit song for Elvis, even though his amazing career had already taken off in 1954-55 with his recording of 19 songs for Sun Records in Memphis. RCA and Elvis would make millions in years ahead.

Haiku Instrumental 1957

To avoid lament
she waters dead plants
and tells me they're dormant.

Inspired by "Li'l Darlin'" by Count Basie and His Orchestra, composed by Neal Hefti, from the great album *The Atomic Basie*. By the second-half of the 1950s orchestra leaders like Duke Ellington, Stan Kenton, Gil Evans, and Gerald Wilson saw and gained popularity and resurgence thanks to the advent of the long play record (a.k.a. LP album or the 33-record). This wonderful, sexy tune gives the listener both a sense of playfulness and longing.

Haiku Song 1957
West Side Suite

(Somewhere Haiku—*Intro*)
If you go to a place called Somewhere
I'll be sure to follow you there.

(Tonight Haiku)
Tonight you slip from sight . . .
you'll become poetry
which I'll hold so tight.

(Somewhere Haiku—*Outro*)
If Somewhere is empty and bare
I'd fill it up with love and dares.

Inspired by the 1957 Broadway musical *West Side Story*, composed by Leonard Bernstein (music) and Stephen Sondheim (lyrics). Like many of America's great Broadway musicals this one remains deep in both our psyche and our archetypal yearning for love, longing, and loss.

Haiku Instrumental 1958

Fighting with haiku rhyme
I'm torn between 'conclude'
and 'some other time.'

Inspired by two instrumentals performed by pianist Bill Evans in December of 1958: "Peace Piece" composed by Bill Evans. And "Some Other Time" composed by Leonard Bernstein, Betty Comden, and Adolph Green. Evans would go on to record this classic ballad throughout his great career.
    My two other favorite Evans versions of "Some Other Time" are: Live at the Village Vanguard June of 1961 (featuring Scott LaFaro on bass) and *The Tony Bennett/Bill Evans Album,* 1975.

Haiku Song 1958

Seasons flip like game-cards,
with each year new
I sometimes think I see you.

Inspired by "Since I Don't Have You," composed and performed by the Doo-Wop group The Skyliners (Jimmy Beaumont, Janet Vogel, Sally Lester, Joe VerScharen and John Taylor). Joe Rock and Lennie Martin also had a hand in composing the song. Doo-Wop is a style of singing using close harmony vocals. As a white group from Pittsburgh with a Soulful sound, this twin river group created a memorable torch ballad. You can hear "Since I Don't Have You" in the motion picture *American Graffiti*, just an hour-and-a-half into the film when actress Cindy Williams foolishly gets into Harrison Ford's Hot Rod. I have been singing this song since my childhood, and I have fond memories of singing out loud in my car "*Youuu, Youuu, Youuu!*" along with lead singer Jimmy Beaumont aching for his love to return.

Haiku Instrumental 1959
Kind of Blue Haikus

[1] So what if the sky's not blue
sometimes I'm better off
without a clue.

[2] Freeloaders over my shoulders,
"hey Sisyphus,
what's this—more boulders!"

[3] Green reef gives in to a blue horizon . . .
things seen in my midseason.

[4] Beyond blue—
Launch me miles
Up into deep space, so I may see
Earth's face.

[5] Sketch me in blue
or soft hue
things which matter
is what drew me to you.

Inspired by all five tracks from Miles Davis' 1959 album masterpiece *Kind of Blue*: "So What," "Freddie Freeloader," "Blue In Green," "All Blues," and "Flamenco Sketches." In my youth, there were two Jazz recordings which led me to my love of this American born music: *Ellington Live at Newport and Kind of Blue*… that simple. All compositions in *Kind of Blue* were composed by Miles and it is regarded as one of the most famous and most influential Jazz recording of all time. What certainly helped Miles create this masterpiece were the accompanying legendary band members:

Miles—trumpet / Julian "Cannonball" Adderley—alto sax
John Coltrane—tenor sax / Bill Evans—piano
Wynton Kelly – (piano on "Freddie Freeloader")
Paul Chambers—bass / Jimmy Cobb—drums

Haiku Song of My Favorite Things 1959

Your tree's my tree,
we hardly disagree,
green tea, black tea,
toast with brie.

Sweet popsicles,
no obstacles,
wow look, icicles on bicycles.

Box-spring under tire swing,
we sing, heart goes zing,
how I love all these things.

Inspired by "My Favorite Things" as performed by Mary Martin (1959) and Julie Andrews (1965). In 1959 a production for *The Sound of Music* was intended as a non-musical Broadway drama about the biography of Salzburg's von Trapp Family Singers which was to feature only two songs as mood-setters. However, Richard Rodger and Oscar Hammerstein II turned *The Sound of Music* into a full-blown musical, creating an iconic phenomenon. Rodger and Hammerstein II were at their peak—at their mountain top—and one can clearly see this as a symbol (or homage) to them in the 1965 film as Julie Andrews opens the motion picture singing the uplifting Prelude "The hills are alive…" on a mountain top. By the time you get to "My Favorite Things" in the film, you will be both singing and dancing along…well, that's what I do every time!

Haiku Instrumental 1960

"What color would you like the room?"
"Are you staying?"
"Yes."
". . . Any color."

Inspired by "Theme From 'A Summer Place'" by Percy Faith and his Orchestra, composed by Max Steiner. One of the most beautiful light classic theme songs to come out of the Rock era with much thanks to the film industry, and one of the most successful instrumentals of the new era. "A Summer Place" was the backdrop for the motion picture of the same title staring Richard Egan, Dorothy McGuire, Troy Donahue, and the very charming Sandra Dee. Even if you've never heard of Percy Faith or seen the movie, I can guarantee you will know this melody. Released in September of 1959, this very popular tune played well into the new decade.

    When I was a child my Granny used to play the record of "A Summer Place" or she would hum it to me just to see my goose-bumps rise; to this day I don't know if it was the attractive melody or Sandra Dee.

Haiku Song 1960

Through winter chill,
wind and rain
one leaf remains . . .
may I have this last dance?

Inspired by "Save The Last Dance For Me," composed by Doc Pomus and Mort Shuman, and performed by The Drifters. In the early 1960s America went nuts for a dance known as the Twist. Dance halls were filled as young folks danced like washing machines! Even though the Twist enabled one to dance singly, your partner was twisting around you and when the romantic ballad came around you would move right in together again, giving rise to a resurgence of romance between partners in the dance. The storyline of "Save the Last Dance for Me" is one of heartbreak, as the love interest is dancing with other suitors, while the only option left is to request a "last wish" to save the last dance. Shakespeare would have approved!

Haiku Instrumental 1961

"Boss, if I take five today,
can I give myself
an hour tomorrow?"

Inspired by "Take Five" by The Dave Brubeck Quartet. Composed by their alto saxophonist Paul Desmond (recorded and first released in late 1959).

    Why is "Take Five" here in 1961? The year 1959 was flooded with history-making music news and record-breaking releases: Miles Davis' *Kind of Blue*; John Coltrane's *Giant Steps*; Buddy Holly killed in a plane accident; Elvis in the Army; Bobby Darin sings "Mac The Knife," Ella Fitzgerald completes the *George Gershwin Songbook*; Motown Records at its infancy; and The Dave Brubeck Quartet attains superstar status with the release of their album *Time Out*. Indeed, all in 1959. Brubeck's *Time Out* circuited the airwaves and local stores for so long that by September of 1961 "Take Five" resurfaced as a 45-rpm single and became an astonishing Pop-crossover hit.

Haiku Song 1961
Journey Reflections I

Friends and loved ones
are like this river—
there's stops and bends
till the trip ends.

Inspired by "Moon River" as performed by iconic actress Audrey Hepburn in the non-musical motion picture *Breakfast At Tiffany's*. Great pre-Beatles music was slim-pickings in the early 1960s, yet there were amazing moments; one of them, for me, is the dreamy-eyed Audrey Hepburn strumming a guitar on a New York City window-ledge singing like a lost migrating bird about a mythical place at the end of a rainbow. Composed by lyricist Johnny Mercer and the master of melody Henry Mancini, who also gave us the film themes for "The Pink Panther," "Charade," "Baby Elephant Walk," "Peter Gunn Theme," "Days of Wine and Roses," and "It's Easy to Say."

Haiku Instrumental 1962

"Grandma,
explain again our solar system?"
"... slice this onion in half..."

Inspired by "Green Onions" by Booker T. & the MG's and composed by most of the members of the group. Okay, okay, so in my haiku I am referring to a standard onion and not the original lovely green long-stem onions... though both onion types make a mean stew! And stew indeed, as early in the 1960s we start to see ethnically integrated music groups. The MGs were well-seasoned musicians and while jamming between a recording session this classic tune was born and swiftly recorded on the spot. The tune became ground zero for the Memphis Sound. Like "Theme From 'A Summer Place'," once you hear "Green Onions" you will know it by its very familiar tune.

ADVISORY: Please be advised when dancing to "Green Onions" your backbone may slip, and this haiku poet and the Booker T. & the MGs are not to be held responsible.

Haiku Song 1962

"Grandpa, are seeds
most important to your farm?"
"No, the morning sun is."

Inspired by two songs: "You Are My Sunshine" composed by Jimmy Davis and Charles Mitchell, and "Lucky Old Sun" composed by Haven Gillespie and Beasley Smith, both as performed by the genius Ray Charles. If Louise Armstrong was the ambassador of Jazz, by the early 1960s Brother Ray had become the ambassador of R&B. However, Ray Charles loved Country Music and in 1962 he proposed the unthinkable to ABC records: to record an album of his favorite Country songs. Executives argued that if he did so he would alienate his R&B and Pop fans. Ray Charles stuck to his druthers and in May of 1962 *Modern Sounds in Country and Western Music* was released, creating a mega-sensation as one of the most important albums of the 20th century. Ray Charles was one of the first black artists to cross over into what was considered "only white-man's music" with a glorious olive branch.

"You Are My Sunshine" was first composed in 1939 and sung by Gene Autry and later by Bing Crosby, but Brother Ray swings his version with an R&B backbone. Decades ago in Southern California when school came to a June close, as summer work I would pick strawberries with the neighborhood kids. We would receive a whopping .75 cents per crate. Work was tough but I did get to sing out loud in an open field, much to my friends' amusement. One of those songs was "Lucky Old Sun," which would have been embarrassing if Brother Ray heard me.

Haiku Instrumental 1963
The Surf Suite

Riding through a tube
surfer's hand on wall
reads the world's double-helix.

Before mammoth waves
and moments of doubt
give yourself time to wipe-out.

Lone surfer on sunset shore
her surfboard's a lighthouse
as tall waves roar.

Inspired by three 1963 surf-rock instrumentals: "Pipeline" by The Chantays, "Wipe Out" by The Surfaris, and "The Lonely Surfer" by Jack Nitzsche. How does one describe incidental music? It is what sets the environment as the listener or viewer experiences a story through music—for example, Purcell's *The Fairy Queen*, Mendelssohn's *Midsummer Night's Dream Music*, Stravinsky's *Rite of Spring*, or Tchaikovsky's *Suite on Romeo and Juliet*. Now jump forward to Los Angeles 1963 and imagine Peter Ilyich Tchaikovsky in tight Speedos taking hold of his long surfboard and shouting out "Okay boys, let's ride the tall ones!" Los Angeles is the ideal California beach scene, wild and often silly, transfixed by the sun, the waves, the hotrods, the bomb fires, and babes! (Oh, I mustn't forget Annette Funicello and Frankie Avalon!)

Washington Haiku Song, August 28, 1963

Hard rains fall,
often clearing all—
seek losses,
use your freedom to call.

Dallas Haiku Song, November 22, 1963

In times of sparse oasis
we drink
of what water leaves us.

Inspired by the song "A Hard Rain's A-Gonna Fall" by Bob Dylan. Songwriter, Singer, Folk Singer, Rock 'n' Roll Artist, Folk-Rock Innovator, Country-Rock, American Roots Music Scholar, and Nobel Prize Winner in Literature—Bob Dylan is all these. Undoubtedly, he is the greatest songwriter of his generation, if not the 20th century. It is as if many of the greatest songwriters of the century funneled their way down through him—Gershwin, Berlin, Porter, Johnson, Guthrie, Williams—all going through him like a great vortex and coming out in the most volatile era: The 1960s!

"A Hard Rain's A-Gonna Fall" comes from his second album, *The Freewheelin' Bob Dylan*, released in May of 1963. The album includes "Blowin' In The Wind," "Masters of War," "Don't Think Twice, It's Alright," "Girl From The North Country," "Bob Dylan's Dream," "Talkin' World War III Blues," and "Oxford Town." If you want to take a "trip" through the 1960s, then you'll need *The Freewheelin'* album as your map. GOOD LUCK!

My two haikus echo the two watershed events of 1963. The first haiku celebrates Reverend Martin Luther King Jr.'s great Peace March on Washington, while the second haiku laments the assassination of President John F. Kennedy. Though Dylan's songs do not mention either one of the two events, we are left with a mood or an emotional connection to things sometimes greater than ourselves.

Haiku Instrumental 1964

Grandma removes her scarf
off the clothesline. . .
bells ring—it's worship time.

Inspired by "*Fegir Nedan* (Call To Worship)" by Hamza El Din, born in Nubia and musically trained in Egypt. In the summer of 1964 Hamza was invited to perform at the Newport Folk festival. He was so well received that the legendary folk record label Vanguard signed him up. "Call To Worship" opens the album, serving as a theme for the illuminating songs that follow, one of which would be noted as his trademark song "*Desse Barama* (Peace)." The year 1964 is amongst the greatest years of music history: The Beatles and the British Invasion, Bossa Nova music from Brazil, John Coltrane's *A Love Supreme* (recorded December 1964), Ravi Shankar's release of three great Raga albums, and Hamza El Din's *Music of Nubia*. And between Ravi and Hamza, the two would help ignite the *World Music* trend.

Haiku Song 1964
The Invasion!

New York sunrays
look like a hand to hold
after a hard night's sadness.

Inspired by "I Want To Hold Your Hand" and "A Hard Day's Night" by The Beatles. Fictional stories are not often written this eloquently as Beatlemania in 1964: In November 1963 we are mourning the loss of a President; the Cold War begins to warm up; casualties start adding up in Vietnam; January 25, 1964 "I Want To Hold Your Hand" becomes a colossal hit, and the single "She Loves You" follows suit. Sunday night, February 9th, 75 million watch The Beatles on The Ed Sullivan Show in New York's NBC Studio! *The British Invasion* is set in motion. In early April, The Beatles monopolize the Pop airwaves with five hit singles. We are only halfway into 1964 when The Beatles released one of the greatest Rock 'n' Roll motion pictures of our era, *A Hard Day's Night*, directed by Richard Lester. The emergence of The Beatles was like Moses splitting the Red Sea, making way for millions upon millions of artists to wade through their craft well into the new millennium.

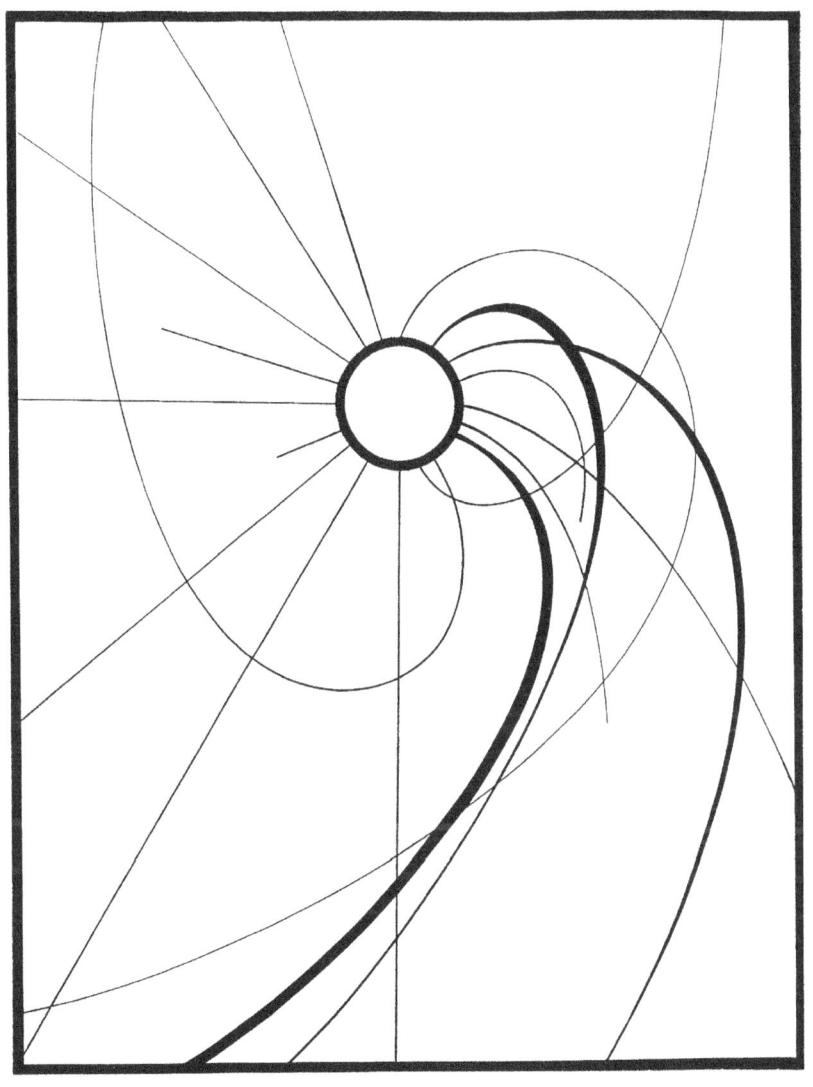

Haiku Instrumental 1965
A Love Supreme Suite

Fell asleep by a river supreme
hissing waters brought
me to dream:

I felt every sea creature
wading the stream
whales, urchins, distant breams.

I heard all animals
along the stream
water, land, and in between.

I saw every bird
slip through a door
shadowing the stream as they soared.

I reached for the cosmos—
pulled down a black-hole net—
the great hunt was set.

With one grand black-hole swoop
I caught them all
as if trapped in a tower.

Yet the net swept all things
from flowers to hours
and all life's world powers.

They struggled to flee
as if my desires
and needs held them with keys.

As I awoke by a tree
swiftly it came to me . . .
all things are free.

Optional Reading by Special Guest Commentator
Cristina Olsen, PhD

Inspired by the instrumental *A Love Supreme* by John Coltrane. Recorded on December 9, 1964, the Jazz suite A Love Supreme was released January 1965. The label included John Coltrane on sax, McCoy Tyner on piano, Jimmy Garrison on bass, and Elvin Jones on drums—all legendary musicians in their own right.

   It usually took John months to compose a piece and record a session. However, it took him only five days to compose *A Love Supreme* and one day to record it. Something profound had happened to John during those five days he sequestered himself in a room of his house. When he reappeared, according to his wife Alice, he was a changed man, both serene and joyful. "This is the first time," he told her, "that I have received all of the music for what I want to record." What John had accomplished was one of the most sublime spiritual meditations in Jazz, which also included a psalm of exaltation for God's presence in his life, printed on the record's jacket. In time, *A Love Supreme* spawned a bevy of Coltrane worshipers with a church dedicated to his name, San Francisco's St. John Coltrane African Orthodox Church.

   However, John was a dedicated student of all religions and rejected the idea that only one religion was right above all others. Every time I listen to John Coltrane's *A Love Supreme*, with John himself briefly chanting the words "a love supreme, a love supreme" in the opening section, I hear the chants of the entire world's religions rolled into one. The tempo of the words unfolds via the musical instruments in different beats and cadences throughout the suite. This is the universal form of chants worldwide, the single and simple phrase gathering levels of complexity and resolving back into simplicity over and over again. In *A Love Supreme*, John takes the chant into a new level of meaning that echoes the spiritual yearnings of the 20th century.

Haiku Song 1965

. . . she removes garden gloves
to make a sign:
"WHO'S CUTTING DOWN OUR FLOWERS?"

Inspired by two songs. The first song, "Where Have All The Flowers Gone?" was originally composed and sung by American Folk icon Pete Seeger. Later, the song would be revised by both Seeger and Joe Hickerson. The power of this song lies in its juxtaposition of images of fallen flowers and fallen soldiers. The partial inspiration for this haiku comes from Johnny River's 1965 version sung with great eloquence in a mournful Folk Rock style.

The second song, "Eve of Destruction," is an anti-war classic composed by P.F. Sloan and Steve Barri and sung by Barry McGuire. The intent of the song was initially bound to be a McGuire B-Side to an upcoming single. The instrumental portion was completed by the famous Wrecking Crew as McGuire laid down a rough vocal. Within a few hours the incomplete demo was found in the Dunhill Records Studio and got into the hands of a local Los Angeles DJ. In early September it became a sensation and by September 25, 1965 McGuire would have his only nationwide hit, with rough mix and all!

Haiku Instrumental 1966

Mercy on the children
and the poor,
some things mustn't be ignored.

Inspired by "Mercy, Mercy, Mercy" by Julian "Cannonball" Adderley's Quintet, composed by Cannonball's pianist Josef Zawinul. Recorded at Capitol Studios October 20, 1966. Music is full of surprises! Imagine in 1966-67 the Beatles working on *Sgt. Pepper's* album while young people were putting flowers in their hair. With Pop rolling over every airwave, Jazz seemed like a thousand light-years away. But Cannonball Adderley rose above all this by simply being cool, really cool! In the 1950s some Jazz musicians created a hip style of Jazz known as Soul Jazz. Now, in the mid-1960s, Cannonballs' Quintet masterfully modernized the Soul Jazz sound for the new Pop listening audience. Listening to the album, also entitled *Mercy, Mercy, Mercy (Live at The Club)*, you can hear how it hops!

Haiku Song 1966
45 rpm A-Side

"Grandma,
what's a good vibration?"
"Well, to live
in a peaceful nation. . .

. . .to help without hesitation
withholding your inner elation. . .

. . .to see World-changing creations
free of deprecation. . .

. . .experience daily rejuvenation
as if mornings are ovations."

Inspired by "Good Vibrations" by The Beach Boys (Brian Wilson and Mike Love). The beloved "Good Vibrations" cost The Beach Boys approximately $16,000 to create, involving 90 hours of studio time and four studios to produce. This would become Brian Wilson's masterpiece single with the Beach Boys (kudos to the Wrecking Crew musicians!) Today it remains on countless music lists as one of the greatest songs ever released.

Haiku Song 1966
45 rpm B-Side

Discovered a lamp
with my freezing hands…
time for me to set a plan!

Wishing for the West
I rub the lamp with my forehead…
my palms get sand.

"California Dreamin'" composed by John Philips of The Mamas and The Papas, echoed beautifully the Californian idealism of The Beach Boys. The group had their beginnings in the East Coast then based themselves in Los Angeles. Their home became a haven for many of the legendary 1960s artists of the time. Cass Eliot (aka Mama Cass) was hands-down the quintessential California dreamer, recognized as matriarch by many who came for music assistance and shelter.

Haiku Instrumental 1967

On ultrasound monitor
their child is pointing
the long road ahead.

Inspired by "Embryonic Journey" by Jefferson Airplane, featuring Jorma Kaukonen on acoustic guitar. Before joining the legendary San Francisco band, Jorma traveled the Folk music circuit until he landed a spot in the Bay Area. Jorma, an accomplished guitarist, fit in perfectly with the Psychedelic Sound rolling in like fog over the Bay. *Surrealistic Pillow* became Jefferson Airplane's apex album and to this day appears often on *best of* lists. Rightly so, the album is like the perfect time travel machine into The Summer of Love. Yet in 1968 all hopes and dreams would shift

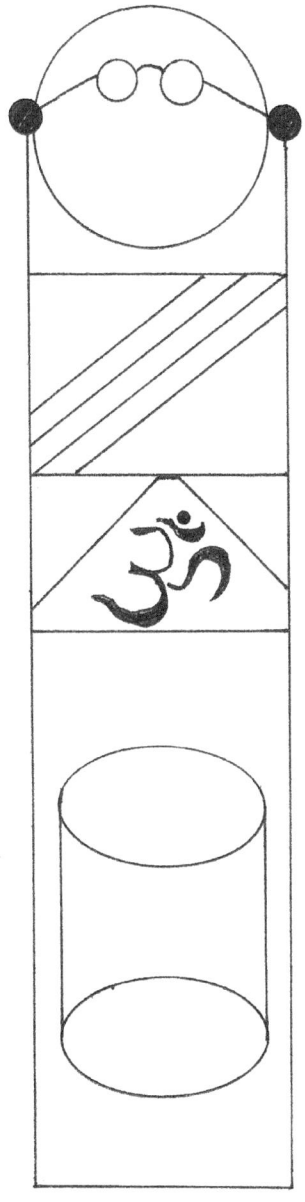

Haiku Song 1967
Pepper Suite

Sergeant please open the
Gate—we'll all sing in
Tune and hope for peace soon.

Pepper the sky with
Endless flowers,
Paint them off your
Palette for hours.

Everyday
Returns: sometimes without words and
Sometimes with: "have you heard . . ."

Looking in a deep
Open hole—
Now see China below.

Eventually our
Little girl will leave
Yet . . . wish the winds would cease.

Hey look
Everyone—the world's a big top . . .
And we can have our own prop!

Rama's bow used for warfare
Till his wife
Sita shot it as a flare.

Can we drink tea from our
Loveseat until the
Universe is complete?

Bathe in morning flowers of light
Before the impending turn of night.

And I heard the
News today . . . the universe is but
Diamonds at play.

A Peppered Note

Inspired by eleven of the thirteen songs from The Beatles masterpiece, *Sgt. Pepper's Lonely Hearts Club Band*. I created my ten haikus in the same chronological order as the album to set a '*Pepper mood*' and without numbering so as not to disrupt my vertical acrostic.
Sgt. Pepper's Lonely Hearts Club Band is considered to be the greatest

recording of the modern era, and after 50 years has lost none of its sparkle. The album's influence is boundless in all aspects: music, lyrics, the album's art, studio innovation, and mass appeal. To this day, the album remains at the top in all the *best of* lists. Countless books, essays, theses, dissertations and film documentaries in many world languages have expressed the love and enthusiasm for this half-century-old masterpiece.

Pepper Songs I utilized for the 10 haikus above are as follows, listed in the same chronological order:

"Sgt. Pepper's Lonely Hearts Club Band" and "A Little Help From My Friends"
"Lucy In The Sky With Diamonds"
"Getting Better"
"Fixing A Hole"
"She's Leaving Home"
"Being the Benefit of Mr. Kite!"
"Within You Without You"
"When I'm Sixty-four"
"Good Morning Good Morning"
"A Day In The Life" and "Lucy In The Sky With Diamond" (*reference*)

Haiku Instrumental Film 1 1968
The Monolith

Light flash
for a brief monolith view . . .
it's but a void as I pass through.

Inspired by *Also Sprach Zarathustra (Thus Spoke Zarathustra)*, Op.30 (1896) by Richard Strauss, as used in Stanley Kubrick's 1968 motion picture *2001: A Space Odyssey*. In 1896 humans hadn't yet mastered aviation let alone space travel! Yet *Also Sprach Zarathustra* was not about searching the *Great Beyond* but rather told a tone-poem of humanity's evolution and Kubrick, a film genius, clearly understood the composition and tells the story in a most remarkable fashion . . . "DAVE, ARE YOU WITH ME...DAVE?..."

Haiku Instrumental Film 2 1968
Una Vida

Cuando vivir es mejor que morir
digo,
"dame este dia."

Inspired by "The Good, The Bad And The Ugly" by Ennio Morricone as performed by Hugo Montenegro and His Orchestra from the 1966 epic film *The Good, The Bad And The Ugly* starring Clint Eastwood, Lee Van Cleef, and Eli Wallach. The Italian "Spaghetti Western" film was a smash in late 1966 and its main theme remained in U.S. theatres and radios long enough to become a major instrumental cross-over hit in April of 1968. Ennio Morricone is clearly one of the giants in the film industry and his music has blessed our ears for over six decades. Extraordinary!

Memphis Haiku Song, April 3, 1968

In awe at mountain top—
it offers much to say
yet I am speechless.

Los Angeles Haiku Song, June 6, 1968

Between the Love-Year and Man-
On-Moon-Year
Bobby's loss brought us to tears.

Inspired by the Jimi Hendrix song "Voodoo Child (Slight Return)." Jimi's opening line: "Well, I stand up next to a mountain…" has forever left an imprint on me. Every time I listen to it I also hear echoes of Martin Luther King Jr.'s last speech in Memphis, April 3, 1968, and I remember Bobby Kennedy's last moments. Though both haikus and events are different in tone, they are very similar in the life-changing impression they make.

   In the 1960s, in that one decade, we witnessed three music pioneers: Bob Dylan, The Beatles (as a group), and Jimi Hendrix. Jimi played his guitar as an extension of his own self. At times the guitar seemed to have a will of its own, creating the song while Jimi channeled through his soul and fingers. Jimi's historical recordings continue to bless us into a new millennium, and we can marvel at his craft through his live performances captured on DVD and TV streaming networks.

My 1968 Story

On a warm afternoon Spring in 1968, I'm a young boy holding a Cesar Chavez grape-protest flag with my grandmother beside me. She is carrying a California flag and an American flag in a shopping bag. The flags are quite small and could easily be mistaken for drink-coasters or handkerchiefs. My grandma places the first stick-poll on the thumb side and the other stick-poll on the pinky side of her hard-worked-hand. Grandma says, "Now my flags look like two fingers making a peace sign!" We both are standing on the corner of Camino Del Sol and Gibraltar Street in my farm town community of Oxnard, California. I ask, "Grandma, is he coming to see Cesar?" She replies, "No, not just him, he is coming to see all of us!" Suddenly a parade of police vehicles and other official cars arrive, and the crowds start cheering. And in the middle of the parade we all see the man—the Kennedy from Massachusetts in the long green convertible heading down Gibraltar Street amongst waves, tears of joy, and euphoric cheers. Grandma then looks down at me and says, "of all the streets in this farming town he chose your uncle's street to go down . . . okay Dave, wave again . . . he is going to be our next President."

Haiku Instrumental 1969
Jimi & Apollo

Apollo man,
please tell us where you walked
and we'll tell you what we've seen.

Inspired by "Star Spangled Banner" by Francis Scott Key (1779–1843), as performed by Jimi Hendrix live at Woodstock on the morning of August 18, 1969. Jimi with his white Fender Stratocaster guitar was about to end his set when he suddenly launched into his rendition of our national anthem, and not just for those who stuck-it-out to see him that Monday morning. Hendrix played our anthem to a nation in deep need of hope, healing, and restoration! True, Jimi had played "Star Spangled Banner" before but never in front of tens-of-thousands. Just a month earlier, U.S. astronauts had made it to the moon with Apollo 11, yet at times their monumental accomplishment seemed over-shadowed by the Vietnam War and global uncertainty. Yet Jimi, a veteran himself, boldly found a way to express beauty, anguish, and something rapturous in just 3:43 minutes of sonic wonder!

Haiku Song 1969
Sea of Tranquility

Your fingers hop across
my bare back . . .
"tell me now how we reached the Moon?"

Inspired by two songs: David Bowie's "Space Oddity," and The Fifth Dimension's "Aquarius/Let The Sunshine In" composed by James Rado, Gerome Ragni, and Galt MacDermot; and thirdly, inspired by the Apollo 11 lunar landing. In 1968 British film director Stanley Kubrick released the motion picture masterpiece *2001, A Space Odyssey,* adding to the fervor of space exploration. Yet, many Pop songs began to appear as early as 1963 with the advent of the NASA Program. In December of 1969 David Bowie's "Space Oddity" was a brilliant example of space travel.

   In April of 1968, when the moon was in the 7th house, the Broadway musical *Hair* moved from its off-Broadway production to the Baltimore Theatre in New York City. The show caused a huge sensation. Looking back, I giggle at the idea of folks going to a show to see "what a hippie really looks like." Off the top of my head, "Aquarius/Let The Sunshine In" has appeared in these four movies: *Woodstock* (as the audience sings "Aquarius/Let the Sunshine In" to deter the rainstorm from pouring down on them, which it did anyway); Milos Forman's film version of *Hair*; the 2001 Walt Disney Picture *Recess: School's Out*; and the 2005 comedy *40 Year Old Virgin*, as Steve Carell and Catherine Keener achieve carnal happiness.

Haiku Instrumental 1970

You read Huxley
and I Herb Caen,
we'll discuss brave worlds over champagne.

Inspired by "Incident At Neshabur" composed by Carlos Santana and guest pianist Alberto Gianquinto, as performed by San Francisco based Latin-Rock band Santana from their sophomore album *Abraxas*. The buzz was everywhere and so was the band. A year earlier their live Woodstock performance became legendary and through hard work and great talent *Abraxas* would become a landmark album, not only for the band but for the 1970s decade. *Abraxas* is regarded as a remarkable achievement fusing Rock and Jazz. A noteworthy alternative version of "Incident at Neshabur," beloved by Santana fans, was recorded live in Japan on the 1973 *Lotus* album—a must listen!

    Last but not least, my haiku also honors the late marvelous San Francisco newspaper columnist Herb Caen, plus I threw in a reference to Aldous Huxley's 1932 book *Brave New World*.

Haiku Song 1970: Part 1

My loved one,
let's make a bridge with our hands . . .
I'm with you till you reach land.

Inspired by "Bridge Over Troubled Water" by Simon & Garfunkel, authored by Paul Simon. On the corner of Glenwood Drive and North C Street in Oxnard, California there is a long established rest-home known as the Glenwood Care Center where my grandma spent her last days in 1976. I walked there every day after school to see her with assorted things to read and an illustrated book of birds. The last thing I remember reading to her was the lyrics to "Bridge Over Troubled Water." This song and the memory of these last moments has stayed with me my whole life, a bridge that will always connect me to my beloved grandmother.

Haiku Song 1970: Part 2

Four scarlet carnations
bloomed today through white snow . . .
blue skies always know.

Inspired by the song "Ohio" by Neil Young (featuring Crosby, Stills & Nash). On May 4th, 1970, during Ohio's Kent State University shootings, four students were killed and 15 wounded by our rifle-wielding American National Guard during a peaceful anti-war protest over the Vietnam War. My reference to red (scarlet), white and blue is to express that behind our American flag we have the freedom to also never forget. It so happens Ohio's State Flower is the Scarlet Carnation (*dianthus caryophyllus*), a beautiful bright red bulbous blossom.

Haiku Instrumental 1971
For Ravi

Krishna played
a ten thousand-year flute dance—
then stopped to play one note: Om . . .

Inspired by "Bangla Dhun" by Ravi Shankar as performed at the benefit *Concert For Bangla Desh* at Madison Square Garden, Sunday, August 1,1971. Concert performances were nothing new to Ravi Shankar as he had been touring the U.S. on many occasions, one of which was his seminal show at The Monterey Pop Festival in the summer of 1967. But what made this show truly special is that on stage sat three of India's greatest musicians: Ravi on sitar, Alla Rakha on tabla, and Ali Akbar Khan on sarod (a deeper-toned sitar). "Bangla Dhun" ran only for sixteen minutes (relatively short for Indian ragas), however those short minutes forever changed my life and set me on my sojourn toward the East in years to follow.

Haiku Song 1971
What's Going On Couplet

Signs for skies—
anti-war lines to shout "why?"
land and sea: things to stand by.

"Place this shell to your ear . . .
hear the sea?"
"No, I hear mercy, mercy me."

Inspired by two songs from the masterpiece album *What's Going On* by Marvin Gaye. "What's Going On" (composed by Marvin Gaye, Renaldo Benson, Al Cleveland), and "Mercy, Mercy Me (The Ecology)" (also by Marvin Gaye). The legendary singer wanted to create a unified concept album consisting of nine song cycles about the Vietnam conflict, the ecology, civil rights, and a struggling world. Motown head Berry Gordy Jr. was not impressed by the album's concept and its pre-production recording sessions, so Gaye himself produced the *What's Going On* album on Motown's Tamla Label and, in my opinion, gave the record company its first surprising masterpiece album! Perhaps most remarkable is Marvin Gaye's voice singing like the archangel Gabriel now reaching across almost half a century since the release of *What's Going On*.

Haiku Instrumental 1972

A babe clutches my finger:
. . . architect, artist,
surgeon, guitarist?

Inspired by "Little Martha," composed by the all-time great guitarist Duane Allman of The Allman Brothers Band. Duane plays this lovely melody accompanied only by fellow guitarist Dicky Betts. Listening to "Little Martha" one can almost smell the sweet Southern magnolias.

Haiku Song 1972

"Grandma,
how did the Rockies appear?"
"Great buffalos once drove earth here."

Inspired by "Rocky Mountain High" by John Denver and co-authored by Mike Taylor. After moving to Aspen, Colorado it took John Denver nine months to finish his classic tune, which for me is one of the most beautiful nature songs ever pressed on record.

Haiku Instrumental 1973

Life is like a magic trick . . .
keep eyes focused,
wait for hocus pocus.

Inspired by "Hocus Pocus" by Focus. OKAY, so I'm guilty as charged! Romp, speed romp went this Dutch rock group right-smack in the middle of the 'Glam Rock' era. This outrageous theatrical music movement lasted a brief 28 months, but there was plenty of time for glittery clothing, cosmic trekking, and outright silliness! Focus members spoke little English, yet it didn't seem to matter here in the States, as this fun instrumental came complete with yodeling, scat singing, whistling, and Jiminy-the-Cricket arias. The first time I heard this song I said, "this is so stupid, loud, extremely fast, a Jethro Tull rip-off, and joyously neurotic! . . . I LOVE IT!"

Here's a fun list of my favorite Glam Rock artists, and some artists that got a little taste of glam glitter, because they simply couldn't stop themselves:

David Bowie / Gary Glitter / Mott The Hoople / Alice Cooper / Sweet / Focus / Roxy Music / Lou Reed / Suzi Quatro / T-Rex / Queen / Brian Eno / David Essex / Elton John / The New York Dolls / Golden Earring / Todd Rundgren / The Raspberries / Slade

Haiku Song 1973
Moon Mood Suite

Don't be
Afraid of what's behind the moon . . .
Reach your minds-eye and make room.

Keep time before
Something ensues,
If you're against a wall, break on through!

Don't be afraid of what's behind
Earth . . . tomorrow, today,
Or rebirth.

Fallen dollars
Trigger men to
Holler, yet kids see new dog collars.

Eager players
Move chess pawns on Swiss cheese
Overlook their expertise.

Orbit the Moon—call me at
Noon, please make it soon and I'll stay attuned.

Inspired by six of the nine songs from Pink Floyd's masterpiece album *Dark Side of The Moon*. My six haikus have been created in chronological order to the original album to set a '*Moon mood*' while still maintaining intact my vertical-acrostic. The six songs were composed (alone or as a group) by Roger Waters, David Gilmour, Richard Wright, and Nick Mason. The songs are: "Breathe In The Air," "Time," "Breathe In The Air (reprise)," "Money," "Us and Them," and "Eclipse." *Dark Side of The Moon* became a sound-scape music marvel and is considered to be one of the greatest recordings to arise from the 1970s.

Haiku Instrumental 1974

Snowflakes on my lawn
like story pieces
from life, death and rebirth.

Inspired by "Pick Up The Pieces" by Average White Band (AWB). In the early 1970's a funky-Rock styled Jazz morphed with the rhythmic style of R&B. It opened the door for Pop Jazz artists like Grover Washington, Chuck Mangioni, The Crusaders, and this Scotland-based band AWB. "Pick Up The Pieces" is so infectious it right away enters your blood and you simply want to snap you fingers and boogie!

Haiku Song 1974

Scorpion treads at water's gate—
we release the lift
and watch it drift.

Inspired by the Stevie Wonder song "You Haven't Done Nothin" from his album *Fulfillingness' First Finale*. Released on August 7, 1974, it features The Jackson 5 on "doo-doo-wop" vocals. Stevie Wonder was clearly one of the greatest artists of the 1970s. He also became one of only a few artists in the Pop/Rock Era to release four masterpieces in a row: *Talking Book* (1972), *Innervisions* (1973), *Fulfillingness' First Finale* (1974), and *Songs In The Key of Life* (1976). Stevie clearly must have been aware of the importance of topical songs similar to his friend Marvin Gaye's *What's Going On* album in 1971. With "You Haven't Done Nothin" Stevie went right for President Richard M. Nixon's jugular. I'm not sure if Nixon ever got the message but just two days after "You Haven't Done Nothin" was released he resigned the Presidency on August 9, 1974.

Haiku Instrumental 1975

As you read prose and verse
let's not lose this
or make time reverse.

Inspired by *The Köln Concert* by pianist Keith Jarrett, one of the most monumental concert recordings of the 20th century that almost did not happen. Jarrett was booked to perform in Köln, Germany but was suffering from exhaustion due to back pain. Nonetheless, he showed up with a back-brace hidden under his clothing, and what followed was a musical performance nothing short of mystical. The solo piano concert uplifts you with its lyricism, pure beauty, and spontaneous rapture as Jarrett's improvisational mastery gives us passage after passage of sonic euphoria (as achieved, for example, at the 7:15 and 10-minute marks into the album).

    In 1975 I was a young music collector willing to listen to anything meaningful. One day I walked into our local Head and Record shop and the store owner said to me, "this Jazz record just came in . . . I think you might like it." He put on the album and out came the first six piano notes that would forever change my life. Me, this scrawny teenager trying to play cool and pretend I was not being affected by such angelic music. But I was hooked! This beloved recording became one of my most treasured discoveries, and like the "Nature Boy" song from 1948, *The Köln Concert* also became my angel, my path, my mantra, and one of the main inspirations leading up to my learning to play the piano.

Haiku Song 1975

Grieving for you on a plane . . .
how a brushfire below
looks like a heart.

Inspired by "Boulder To Birmingham" by Emmylou Harris, featured in the album *Pieces of The Sky*. In the history of music there has always been legendary tales of artists who single-handedly created their own myth by either falling from grace or shooting to the stars. Here is a story of two star-struck music artists where one ascended as the other descended, much in the vein of the archetypal tale as told in the film *A Star Is Born*. Country-Rock legend Gram Parsons and a young Emmylou Harris paired up to collaborate on the album GP, which was released to moderate sales. Yet Parsons and Harris pressed on with what little money they had and went on a music tour to raise funds for Parsons' second album. The two worked tirelessly on it, yet as Emmylou became more and more invested in Parsons' artistry, he in turn slid deeper into alcohol and drug addiction. In late 1973 their album *Grievous Angel* was completed, but Parsons died before he would ever see this seminal album. In 1974 this groundbreaking album became a sensation and the only spokesperson for the album was Emmylou Harris, along with her grief.

    By 1975 Emmylou would go solo under the direction of producer Brian Ahern. In February *Pieces of The Sky* became one of Country-Rock's greatest achievements. It features "Boulder To Birmingham," the song she began composing for Gram Parsons while mourning his loss, and Bill Danoff was credited as shared composer. This song is so beautifully heart wrenching, filled with longing, loss and denied desire that every word hits a deep emotional cord.

Haiku Instrumental 1976

I've counted prayer beads for years
   yet nothing comes close
      to when you're near.

Inspired by *Music for 18 Musicians* by Steve Reich. This 60-minute hypnotic work premiered on April 24, 1976 at The Town Hall in New York City. The work consists of 14 parts with a steady pulse moving ever so gently through the melodies with no break in between. This Classic-experimental style of music was first titled *The New York Hypnotic School* (based in SoHo) but later, with modern composers like Terry Riley, Philip Glass, LaMonte Young, and Steve Reich, the term came to be known as Minimalism. What makes this style so remarkable are the roots of its origins. Almost all Minimalist composers were devotees of Johann Sebastian Bach of some 300 years ago! Listen close and you can hear counterpoint, melodic-rounds, and fugues all whapped into a 20th century heartbeat.

Haiku Song 1976

"Hudson sailboats look like butterflies."
"No, it's a pizza slice with flies."

PLUS!

Hey-ho, A Bonus Haiku So Silly, I Couldn't Let It Go!

"Hey-ho, see the van Gogh."
"Where was it towed?"
"A shop in SoHo."
". . . Let's go!"

Inspired by "Blitzkrieg Bop" by The Ramones. Another great music moment from the 1970s was the arrival of the New York-based Punk rock band that consisted of DeeDee Ramone, Johnny Ramone, Tommy Ramone, and lead singer Joey Ramone, arriving not with lovely-touchy songs but with sonic Molotov cocktails shouting "HEY-OH, LET'S GO!"

NO FEAR, NO NEED TO LOCK YOUR HOUSE. Though the Ramones almost singlehandedly started the Punk movement, their songs were not overtly violent in nature or crude; on the contrary, they were funny, joyous, playfully political, and cynical. What scared most of mainstream America was that The Ramones were a counter reaction to the jet-setting Disco scene and corporate Rock so prominent at the time. There were no limos or huge million dollar contracts; for the Ramones there was only CBGBs, the legendary Punk nightclub on East 2nd Street. They played loud and very fast with most songs clocking at under 2:30 minutes.

FOR JOEY AND PIZZA: The 'pizza' reference comes from the 1979 motion picture *Rock 'n' Roll High School* starring P.J. Soles and The Ramones. The film was a teen-exploitation romp complete with mayhem, bad dialogue, and a lot of *CHEESE!* One of the best scenes in the movie happens when Joey Ramone is denied pizza and force-fed wheat-germ. From that moment on Joey and pizza were synonymous.

Haiku Instrumental 1977

Sailing—
adrift and at peace,
bliss just happens when you expect it least.

Inspired by "Warszawa" by David Bowie and co-authored by Brian Eno, from Bowie's timeless album *LOW* released in 1977. "Warszawa" was based on a trip Bowie had made to Poland back in 1973. Bowie and Eno produced half of the material for *LOW* in 1976 while in Berlin. Bowie had become majorly attracted to the Ambient Music movement, and thus *LOW* contained mainly pop songs on side one of the record and ambient pieces on side two. "Warszawa" and the album *LOW* would become extremely influential in years to come.

Haiku Song 1977

Black and white birds
look like piano keys on a wire
till notes fly off.

Inspired by "Songbird" by Fleetwood Mac, composed and performed by Christine McVie. In April of 1977 Fleetwood Mac's *Rumours* album became a huge sensation. This iconic album almost didn't happen. After the success with their 1976 album entitled *Fleetwood Mac*, internal relationships among the band members spun out of control and breakups and divorces ensued. Nonetheless, the band plowed through their emotions during the production phase to create a 1970s classic. Among them is Christine's song "Songbird," performed live in the empty hall of the Zellerback Auditorium at the University of California, Berkeley.

Haiku Instrumental 1978

Departing from your
hometown airport
among souvenirs,
years and tears.

Inspired by *Ambient 1: Music For Airports* by Brian Eno. In 1975 Brian Eno created a landmark Ambient record with *Discreet Music*. While recovering from an automobile accident which kept him in bed for a spell, one day Brian Eno heard Classical harp music playing, but unable to turn up the volume from his bedside he became conscious of an array of other sounds in his environment interweaving with the music. Thus began the Ambient movement. This was not the first instance of ambient music. At the turn of the century French composer Erik Satie coined a type of ambient music as "furniture music." Eno experienced music much the same way: to create music as *muzak* it is not required to sit and listen but rather to allow it to quietly flow ever so gently in the background. His idea was well taken; however people did indeed listen deeper into the Ambient structures, and the impact of this music created a huge wave that ever-so-gently continues to wash upon our shores to this day!

Haiku Song 1978

"You're a nice guy—
what a nice date . . .
are you vegan?"
"Yes, I eat fruit-rolls."

Inspired by "Germfree Adolescents" by London-based band The X-Ray Spex, composed and performed by lead singer Poly Styrene. I couldn't wait for 1978 to come around and bow to Poly and this wonderful London-based band. Poly Styrene, the braces-wearing British Punk Rocker, was of tiny stature but ROCKED WITH GUSTO! Styrene, whose real name was Marianne Joan Elliott-Said, created social commentary songs that reflected consumerism, sexism, and negative-media long before the "You Tube" generation. Poly was a true powerhouse in a male-dominated forum. The X-Ray Spex 1978 release of "*Germfree Adolescents*" is a modern day classic that continues to influence many rockin' women of our day!

The 1970s saw some amazing women in rock. Along with Poly, here are more of my favorite Rock Girls:

Patti Smith
Debbie Harry (of Blondie)
Suzi Quatro
Gaye Advert (of The Adverts)
Pauline Murray (of Penetration)
Chrissie Hynde (of The Pretenders)
Exene Cervenka (of X)
Penelope Houston (of The Avengers)
The Slits
The Runaways
Tina Weymouth (of The Talking Heads)
Kate Pierson and Cindy Wilson (of The B-52's)
Siouxie and The Banshees
The Morgans
Lene Lovich
Lydia Lunch

Haiku Instrumental 1979

Your body flows
like a strait . . .
I think of you over the Golden Gate.

Inspired by "It's Easy To Say" composed by Henry Mancini as a solo piano piece for the motion picture *10* and performed by Dudley Moore.

How could this have happened?" Sometimes when viewing mediocre movies we hope for a valid reason as to why we showed up to see the thing in the first place! In 1979 film director Blake Edwards released *10*, a romantic farce that had few laughs and poor plot. Yet Edwards could always depend on Henry Mancini to create great film scores for him as he did in the past, for example, *The Pink Panther* films. I had adored Mancini's music since childhood and this was no exception. The wonderful British comedian Dudley Moore had the starring role, and along with being a great comedic actor he was an accomplished pianist. In the film we find Moore in a Hawaiian bar exquisitely playing "It's Easy To Say" on a grand piano for an audience of only two people. For me, "It's Easy To Say" was one of the most beautiful ballads I had ever heard. It took me many years to teach myself to play this 3-minute piano-gem. "It's Easy To Say" is not easy to play—but it's easy to love.

Haiku Song 1979

One drop of rain
can change my day
as one artist's work
can lead the way.

Inspired by "One Drop" and "So Much Trouble In The World," both by Bob Marley. In the 1970s Bob Marley stands with great distinction amongst the 1960s pioneers that shaped music well into the new millennium, a musical genius who revolutionized the once local reggae genre into a worldwide phenomenon. Bob Marley achieved this goal by giving us songs of compassion, love, social justice, social awareness, and deep-rooted spiritual themes.

Haiku Instrumental 1980

I sought to reverse time
    to save you,
now I take time
    to think of you.

Inspired by "Theme from *Somewhere In Time*" by film composer John Barry from the motion picture *Somewhere In Time,* a romantic-fantasy drama which takes the main character, Christopher Reeve, from the 1980s back to the turn of the century to fall in love with a stage actress played by Jane Seymour. This is one of my favorite films, perhaps for its hypnotic sentiment and musical resonance with the Acoustic Era (1890-1922). What is most thrilling about the film is the beautifully moving soundtrack, thanks to John Barry paying homage to the last great Romantic Classical composer, Rachmaninoff, incorporating into the film his *Rhapsody on a Theme of Paganini*.

Haiku Song 1980
A Double Fantasy Suite

The sound of Beatles at a flea market . . .
bargain records for a lifetime.

The sound of Koto drums in forests . . .
a lone cricket in the desert.

The sound of your heartbeat upon me . . .
our love is every fantasy.

Inspired by three songs from the album *Double Fantasy* by John Lennon, released November 19, 1980. The songs are: "Watching The Wheels," "Dear Yoko," and "Woman."

When I was a young man, my folks would drive me to the Simi Valley Flea Market. My lawn mowing money would be spent on model electric trains, music records, and Beatles memorabilia. As I began creating haikus for *The Double Fantasy Suite*, I looked back at myself as that scrawny 90-pound kid who looked like a popsicle stick with tumbleweed-hair, walking up to vendors and sheepishly asking for pictures of John and George. They probably didn't see me as a "cool kid," but goodness, I was a tenacious one.

Years later, the shock of John Lennon's death catapulted me on an existential journey which lasted years (some say, I'm still walking that journey). By utter serendipity, on that fateful night of December 8, 1980, I was having a Beatles gathering where friends and collectors traded Beatles music. That very evening I was creating a master tape of bootleg Beatles. And then the tragic news broke. I saw the world with different eyes then, saw how fate sometimes has a way of testing a path's terrain far greater than ourselves. Overnight I transitioned from being an exuberant child to a reflective person.

Haiku Instrumental 1981
A Child's Second Letter To Earth

"Full moon below the South Pole,
for what it's worth
please keep a light on Earth."

Inspired by *The Goldberg Variations* by Johann Sebastian Bach, as performed and recorded by pianist Glenn Gould in late 1981 and issued by Columbia Records in 1982. As I mentioned in my 1955 Haiku, Glenn Gould would return and recreate music history in 1981. His CD received countless accolades and awards, yet Gould would ride the wave for a few months before his abrupt death.

Haiku Song 1981
The Clock Watcher

9, bridge fee
10, coffee
12, meeting
1, dreaming
3, drink tea
5, flee!

Inspired by Dolly Parton's "9 To 5." How she could sing, compose, arrange and entertain! Yet for me, what makes her truly a remarkable artist is her songbook canon. With her authenticity and individual tenacity in the competitive Country/Pop world of Nashville and the South, she stands as an icon! Dolly composed "9 To 5" and sang the title-song for the smash comedy motion picture of the same title, co-starring Jane Fonda and Lily Tomlin. The three of them had an absolute ball and you can really see it in this joyous film. Dolly said, "in the film I simply played myself…" And certainly it worked, as it has throughout her remarkable career!

Haiku Instrumental 1982
A Winter Tale

I drive you through snow—
speechless you draw a heart shape
on the car windshield.

In a white landscape
you build a snowman
with wide-eyes—missing a mouth.

Silently driving home . . .
white earth against skies of blue
you say, "thank you."

Inspired by "Thanksgiving" by composer-pianist George Winston from his platinum album *December*. In 1976 acoustic guitarist William Ackerman and art designer Anne Robinson founded Windham Hill Records. At first the music industry didn't know how to label this kind of "new" type of music, but Bay Area Tower Records provided Windham with a music section in their stores and by 1982 pianist George Winston's albums began to sell like mad, thus sparking the New Age music genre. In 1982 Winston would release two albums: *Winter In Spring* and his masterful *December*. Winston's beautiful solo piano albums would become one of the top selling labels of the 1980s decade!

Haiku Song 1982
Nebraska Suite

Watching movies
in our van
we missed seeing The Grand Canyon.

Playing video games
on a plane
I missed seeing Mt. Rushmore.

Texting my therapist
in the car
I never saw that tree.

Inspired by the song "Used Cars" and other assorted songs from Bruce Springsteen's acoustic masterpiece *Nebraska*. Bruce recorded the Nebraska songs in elated sparseness on a Teac Portastudio 4-track cassette-tape machine in his home. With *Nebraska* Bruce channeled American Roots Music from the deepest core, landing unexpectedly at a time when folk music had been shelved like a by-gone genre, and in spite of the New Wave, sparking a resurgence of the folk and folk-rock movement.

Haiku Instrumental 1983

My journey's not about grandeur
or money—
it's the long harmony.

Inspired by "An Ending (Ascent)" by Brian Eno, from the album *APOLLO: Atmospheres, Space and Soundtracks* (also featuring Daniel Lanois and Brian's brother Roger Eno). This glorious soundtrack was released in the summer of 1983. The three musicians managed to truly capture the feel of the cosmos as each track guided the listener through various space odysseys, allowing one to float in the heavens while in the safety of one's own couch. "An Ending (Ascent)" has appeared in many motion pictures and at various memorial openings.

Haiku Song 1983
Study In Synchronicity

Monk drops prayer beads in a church—
they land on a centipede below.

Young infant drops a chicken-nugget—
it lands in his dog's mouth below.

Man flicks cigarette from a car—
it lands by tobacco fields below.

Eagle fumbles the catch of the day—
fish lands back in the water below.

Child lets a park balloon go—
it pops on a wire and drops far down below.

Inspired by "Synchronicity 1" and "Synchronicity 2" by The Police, composed by Sting. Also inspired by Maurice Nicoll's book *Living Time And The Integration Of The Life*.

    In 1979 The Police trio entered stardom with their punk style mixed with Rock 'n' Roll and Reggae. By 1982-83 they had incorporated Jazz-fusion and New Wave. At this time lead songwriter and singer Sting went through a painful divorce that sent him on a soul-searching journey. Much of the Synchronicity album is attributed to his inner search and his growing interest in Jungian psychology.

    In my studies of religious symbols in the late 1970s I discovered the psychology of Carl Jung through his book *Man And His Symbols*. Shortly after *Synchronicity* was released in 1984 I discovered Maurice Nicoll's book *Living Time And The Integration Of The Life*. A student of Jung, as well as Gurdjieff and Ouspensky, Nicoll proposed that time was not just an abstract, symbolical representation of movement and change, but an actual living entity. Both *Synchronicity* and *Living Time* deepened profoundly my spiritual view of reality.

Haiku Instrumental 1984

Trout in a stream
in a rainbow-like gleam—
some things are better than dreams.

Inspired by "A Stream With Bright Fish" by Harold Budd and Brian Eno from the Ambient masterpiece *The Pearl*. Released in 1984, when the world continued to explore outer space in search of a greater "apple," Budd and Eno gave us one of the most "deep-water" recordings of the 20th century. *The Pearl*'s ambient theme explores the deep oceans and its aquatic mysteries. California-based composer Harold Budd, with a strong background in Classical training, delivers stunning melodies to the Ambient landscape or "water-scape" of the *Pearl*.

Haiku Song 1984

My first date as a "lady thriller" . . .
why did I splash on
weed killer?

Inspired by "Thriller," composed by Rod Temperton and performed by Michael Jackson. In November of 1982 Michael Jackson's *Thriller* album became a world phenomenon. To this day it remains one of the highest selling recordings. From 1982 to 1984 the *Thriller* album generated an astonishing seven singles, with the single "Thriller" being the last to grace the nation with his final hit in February of 1984. Highly worth viewing is Jackson's 14-minute groundbreaking music video directed by John Landis.

Haiku Instrumental 1985

Our kids are kittens
with nose in milk cartons,
and the day's just startin'.

Inspired by "Scuttle Buttin'(1985 live version)" by Stevie Ray Vaughan. Stevie Ray's triumphant return to the "Montreux Jazz Festival" in 1985 was one of music's greatest moments. Stevie first appeared in Montreux in 1982 to a crowd of boos. Though his performance was outstanding, few seemed to be "listening" to his masterful guitar playing. In 1984 Stevie became a phenomenon with his release of *Couldn't Stand The Weather*. On July 16, 1985 he walked onto the Monteux stage again and the audience went bonkers! His opening track was "Scuttle Buttin'" one of the fastest played, joyful blues songs I have ever heard! It leaves you wondering how anyone can play this fast in a live performance. . . . Stevie Ray wasn't just "anyone."

Haiku Song 1985
Space Shuttle Tragedy of 1986

"Grandma, let's challenge this hill—
climb up far,
and bring back those falling stars."

Inspired by the song "Running Up That Hill" by Kate Bush, October of 1985, and by the Space Shuttle Challenger tragedy, January 28, 1986.

British musician-songwriter Kate Bush released her *Hounds of Love* album with stunning overlay of sound and theatrical intent. As a music collector I often compare myself to a miner digging up rare stones and gems and every once in a while that rare gold nugget. And Kate Bush's *Hounds of Love* is indeed one of my personal favorite "nuggets," an opus that never fails to fill me with joy and rapture.

I recall that just moments after the Space Shuttle Challenger tragedy "Running Up That Hill" was playing on the radio. By odd coincidence, in her song "Hello Earth," also featured on *Hounds of Love*, we can hear an official tape from Houston conversing with astronauts in space. Little did Kate know how immersed she and the world had become with space travel and the price to be paid.

Haiku Instrumental 1986
Give Them Names

A lone bell tolls
In our home,
Don't feel shamed—
Save the dead and give them names.

Inspired by "Home" by British artist David Sylvian from his CD *Gone To Earth*, released September 1986. The CD consisted of one part atmospheric vocals and the other part of ambient pieces. He had some good friends helping him out: Robert Fripp of King Crimson and Bill Nelson of Be-Bop Deluxe.

    By the mid-1980s we were struggling to come to grips with the AIDS epidemic. I once knew a brilliant and strong man who worked as a telephone specialist just as the wireless phone era was approaching. He worked in Washington DC, in the White House, in the halls of Congress, and the great Federal buildings which reflect our freedom and civic tolerance. One day he found himself growing sickly and weak. He asked for help but received none. Eventually he ended up back home in the care of Hospice in California. That strong man was my beloved cousin Danny Muñoz who died in the arms of his father, who loved him free of shame.

Haiku Song 1986

Lunar New Year's firecrackers
in thunderous applause
makes a red rain.

Inspired by "Red Rain" by Peter Gabriel. In the late 1960s Gabriel was one of the founding members of the British Progressive-Rock group Genesis, yet by 1975 Gabriel headed for a solo career. Gabriel's greatest success came in 1986 with his classic album *So*. "Red Rain" opens the album with world beats soaked in a "rain-like" melody. His album So would also generate three U.S. hits: "Sledgehammer," "Big Time," and "In Your Eyes."

For me, one of the most memorable moments in 1980s cinema is in the coming-of-age film *Say Anything* when hopeful character Lloyd, played by John Cusack, holds up a shoulder-wide boom-box playing Peter Gabriel's "In Your Eyes" for love-interest Diane Court (Iona Skye). It all seems a little cliché but inescapably romantic.

Haiku Instrumental 1987
Ravi and George

"Monsoon looms."
"How's that?"
"The park money is storing pears
in earthenware."

Inspired by "Friar Park" by Ravi Shankar (featuring George Harrison). As the 1980s New Wave music trend was sweeping the globe, Indian Classical artist Ravi Shankar thought of the idea of making a "crossover" album. To embark on such a project Ravi asked his spiritual son, George Harrison, to help him contribute to his CD *Tana Mana*. George was so delighted he invited Ravi to his home (with top-of-the-line studio) at George's Friar Park estate.

    The "monkey" reference pertains to my favorite Hindu mythology character: Hanuman, the monkey god and utter devoted friend of Lord Rama and his wife Sita. In the epic story Hanuman is asked by Rama to save Sita who is trapped in the south of India, known today as Sri Lanka. It is here that the monkey god builds a bridge between the two lands to escort the goddess back to safety. This haiku serves as a modern-day metaphor of the friendship that existed between Ravi and George. . .a bridge indeed.

Haiku Song 1987

Monk's hands glow
against a lone candle . . .
he says, "It's time."
And blows it out.

Inspired by "With Or Without You" from the album *The Joshua Tree* by the Dublin-based group U2. First as Post-Punkers and then New Wavers, U2 was popular on 1980s FM radio and on college campuses. Then in 1984 U2 released *Unforgettable Fire*, which contained the anthem-like tribute to Rev. Martin Luther King Jr., "Pride (In The Name of Love)." In 1987 U2 released their masterpiece album, *The Joshua Tree*. To this day *The Joshua Tree album* appears on "best of" lists, marking U2's apex.

Haiku Instrumental 1988

I hold you in my dreams—
sunrise comes
and things aren't what they seem.

Inspired by "With This Love" by Peter Gabriel, from his album *Passion*, soundtrack for Martin Scorsese's film *The Last Temptation of Christ*. In the fall of 1989 the film caused some controversy, yet Peter Gabriel's music did not. Listeners were attracted to the World Beat rhythms and instrumentation used in the score. "With This Love" is presented in two parts, the first with small ensemble and the second with small ensemble and a boys' wordless choir. Both are magical! Gabriel began recording the soundtrack in 1988 and the *Passion* CD was released in the Fall of 1989 along with the film. So don't get *hung up* on the film; enjoy the music… no pun intended.

Haiku Song 1988

Voltaire, make us aware,
Earth's to share . . .
we'll put up signs: "HANDLE WITH CARE."

Inspired by The Traveling Willbury's "Handle With Care." Musician/producer Jeff Lynn and legendary singer Roy Orbison were over at ex-Beatle George Harrison's house in Los Angeles helping him flesh out a melody he had playing in his head. Extra help was needed. First stop was over to Tom Petty and his many extra guitars, then over to Bob Dylan where luck would have it Bob had 10 days free to record with them, and thus the magic began! The record release of the masquerading band of brothers became a triumphant success, filled with great musical joy and song-writing

Haiku Instrumental 1989

Home:
warm bath, fire, tea, blankets—
outside snow falls . . .
shit, my car lights are on!

Inspired by "Mad Rush" by Philip Glass, from his masterful CD *Solo Piano*. Glass went back to his first roots of playing solo—something he had achieved with great success during his New York City days in the late 1960s and early 1970s. Please don't let the song title fool you – "Mad Rush" is a 13-minute mesmerizing journey of the soul.

Haiku Song 1989
The Berlin Wall Suite

"Grandma, what are hammers for?"
"To fix floors
and break down walls for new doors."

"Sister, through the other side
flowers ignite!"
"Break down the wall, give them light."

"Brother, hear cheers
over the wall?"
"Let's paint 'FREEDOM' on the wrecking ball!"

Inspired by Neil Young's "(Keep on) Rockin' In The Free World" and "Wrecking Ball" from his CD *Freedom*. Released in October 1989, "Rockin'..." seems to foretell the demolition of the Berlin Wall on November 9, 1989. It was "Rockin' In The Free World" indeed! The second song is a ballad about going to a dance in a fictitious palace known as the "The Wrecking Ball." Prophetic and poetic, is it not?

Haiku Instrumental 1990

"Can this Buddha statue
with butter cup feed land and sea?"
"Look, a bee . . ."

Inspired by *Raga Kedara* by Ustad Bismillah Khan. (*Ustad* means "master" or "great teacher.") Bismillah Khan's instrument was a *shehnai* (an Indian reed-like oboe). He had lived to be 90 years old and played almost up to his death in 2006, long enough to become one of India's national treasures. I have loved his music since my youth, and of his 30 recordings in my library half of his CDs have been imported from India. Most ragas run about 45 to 70 minutes in length, so the advent of CDs in the 1980s was well suited to Classical Indian Raga recordings because it was no longer necessary to disrupt the piece after only 22-minutes of playing in order to turn over the LP.

Haiku Song 1990
Journey Reflections II

It's not about the end—
it's about road bends
and journeys left by friends.

Inspired by the song "Here's Where The Story Ends" by The Sundays, composed by David Gavurin and Harriet Wheeler. Popular music was diving into the Alternative Rock 'n' Roll revolution filled with raves, sweat, blood, ecstasy and *mosh pits*. Meanwhile, the London-based group The Sundays took their own spin on the "alternative-style sound" revolution with soft edges and leisurely melodies so hypnotically beautiful. Clearly, great women musicians lead the way through the 1980s well into the 1990s, composing their own music, backed by male musicians or mixed bags in general.

Here are some of my favorite late 1980s and 1990s boys-with-leading-ladies or all-girl-groups:

The Go-Go's
10,000 Maniacs
Cocteau Twins
The Shop Assistants
The Cranberries
The Breeders
The Innocence Mission
The Softies
Saint Etienne
Stereolab
Cardigans
L7
Sixpence None The Richer
Camera Obscura
Lone Justice
Sky Cries Mary
The Sugarcubes (featuring Björk)
Rilo Kiley (featuring Jenny Lewis)

Haiku Instrumental 1991: *Two Brothers*

Brother,
you held prayer beads like stones
not to be alone to atone.

And I broke prayer beads
like stringed pearls,
then dove in to give life a whirl.

To my soul brother Jaime "Chocalé" Becerra

Inspired by *Fratres Music for Strings and Percussion,* 1991 version (first version recorded in 1977) by Arvo Pärt. Around 1985 my monastic friend and music theory tutor Jaime *"Chocalé"* Becerra handed me this very sublime music piece. Now jump forward three decades later. While my friend Jaime dug into the monastic track, in 1985 I went rogue far from the church; and yet, as I still listen to this piece I am filled with mixed emotions of love, prayer, companionship, roads not taken, and other roads taken which lead into landscapes of spiritual understanding, where rivers divide and mountains are seen apart from each other.

 The composer, Arvo Pärt, was born in Paide, Estonia just before WWII. His Modern Classic schooling gave him an advantage with his deep insight into the "spiritual." *Fratres* means "brothers," and the music indeed draws us into something greater than ourselves. In the 1991 version the percussion section ever-so-gently taps "1,2,1,2" as if something is knocking in the thin air to prepare us.

 On Saturday, October 6, 2012, my wife Cristina and I attended a performance of *Fratres* at the San Francisco Symphony. Through the 10-minute duration of the piece Cristina held my hand as she gently tapped on my palm with her finger along with the music. It was her way of fostering me through an ever changing spiritual landscape.

Haiku Song 1991

Spider caught in its own web,
removes leg
and gets on with seven.

Inspired by "Losing My Religion" by R.E.M from their album *Out of Time*. By the time the album was released the group had signed onto a huge record label, yet they miraculously contained total control of their creativity. *Out of Time*, filled with pop tunes and folk-rock styled songs, came as quite a surprise to fans (I being one of them). The album did feature three R.E.M. classic songs, "Country Feedback," "Shiny Happy People," and "Losing My Religion." The first time I heard this exuberant song I started dancing on the top parking lot floor at San Francisco State University where as a student I worked as a parking attendant, singing the song with great vibrato! That was the extent of my "wild" college days.

Haiku Instrumental 1992

Old Miss feeds New Orleans
in her splendor
for this there's no surrender.

Inspired by "New Orleans Instrumental No.1" by R.E.M. With this gentle flowing tune one can imagine a riverboat heading toward the historic city. In 1982 and the early 1990s the Georgia-based Rock band R.E.M. produced consistently wonderful music. In September 1992 R.E.M. released their masterpiece album entitled *Automatic For The People*. Throughout the century countless songs have been created regarding the Mighty Mississippi flowing into the great known and unknown. For fun, revisit my haiku songs from 1918 and 1919.

Haiku Song 1992
From Years of Interviewing School Kids Alike

I don't want to get old
and toss my kite
mom and dad, that just ain't right."

. . . don't want to get old
and kiss a girl
that's worse than spinach—makes me hurl.

. . . don't want to get old
and kiss a guy
that's worse than measles—you try.

. . . don't want to get old
and lose my Barbie shape—
next thing—I'm a big grape.

. . . don't want to get old
and be a real man
I'm just fine being Peter Pan.

. . . don't want to get old
and go to work
when I hear dad say, "…guy's a jerk!"

Inspired by "I Don't Wanna Grow Up" by Tom Waits and is wife Kathleen Brennan. I have been a huge fan of Tom Waits since his debut album in 1973. In 1992 Tom was at the height of what I coin his "theatrical period" with the release of *Bone Machine*, an album so spooky, so sinister, and often howling with dog-like expression that it would scare the inner-child right out of anyone. Yet the quirkiness that always lies behind his heightened sense of humor makes it all OK. "I Don't Wanna Grow Up" is one of Tom's classic tunes, turning a childhood sing-along into a hilarious social commentary!

Haiku Instrumental 1993
The Four

Earth Goddess statue
with lichen and bird droppings. . .
life isn't stopping.

Inspired by "Mother Goddess" by Ali Akbar Khan. In 1993 Khan released *Garden of Dreams,* an "east meets west" fusion CD (much like Ravi Shankar's *Tana Mana* CD in 1987). Khan, deeply embedded in Classical Raga roots, created only two fusion recordings that I know of in his amazing career. The Western theme was something he could not avoid, as he founded The Ali Akbar Khan College of Music in Marin County, California. I had the pleasure of meeting Ali Akbar Khan in 1990-91 as I was teaching myself the Indian harmonium. He asked me how I found playing the keyboard instrument and I sheepishly replied, "it's difficult . . ." I think we understood each other. Ali Akbar Khan is my last Indian inductee into this book of haikus. For me, the most influential Classical Indian musicians are Ravi, Bismillah, Ali, and Alla. In the West we have our Classical heroes Bach, Mozart, Beethoven, and Brahms, all from closely-knit but different periods in history. But in 20th century India they had all four living entities on this earth at the same time! Three of the members often played together (Ravi, Ali and Alla), most notably during the benefit *Concert For Bangla Desh*. All four were pioneers in their craft and all four opened many doors to millions of musicians from India and to the world at large.

THE FOUR:
Alla Rakha on tabla (1919–2000)
Bismillah Khan on shehnai (1916–2006)
Ali Akbar Khan on sarod (1922–2009)
Ravi Shankar on sitar (1920–2012)

Haiku Song 1993

Silk, skin, captured grin, things within,
hair through fingers—
oh, how you linger.

Inspired by "Linger" composed by Dolores O'Riordan and Noel Hogan of The Cranberries. Britain and Ireland's love of sonic-pop music was everywhere during the 1980s and well into the early 1990s. However, with the "grunge-movement" from Seattle sweeping the music world, The Cranberries took the sonic-Brit-sound and added melodic textures with slight Celtic overtones to help lead them to stardom. Their first album, *Everybody Else Is Doing It, So Why Can't We?* swept the U.K. but what caught America's ear was the amazing break-up ballad "Linger." The song would become a classic radio favorite and is often played on FM radio even today (…that's if you own a radio).

Haiku Instrumental 1994

Geometric lands
shaped with our hands
till we succumb with parting sands.

Inspired by "The Great Gig In The Sky" (1994 *Live Pulse Version*) from London's Earl's Court by Pink Floyd (music by Rick Wright and vocal composition by Clare Torry.) In March of 1973 British Rock band Pink Floyd released their masterpiece *Dark Side of The Moon*. Twenty-one years later, in 1994, the band challenged themselves to perform the entire *Dark Side of The Moon* live. In their live CD entitled *Pulse* (also a DVD), Rick Wright and guitarist David Gilmore employed not one but three women vocalizing through the piece. Performers Sam Brown, Claudia Fontaine, and Durga McBroom are magnificent in pouring out so much emotion with so much dynamic music.

Haiku Song 1994

Elders with different stories
met at the plateau
with new things to show.

Inspired by "Plateau" covered by Nirvana, originally composed by the rock band The Meat Puppets. This live version of "Plateau" featured in Nirvana's *MTV Unplugged* in New York from their 1994 CD.

After the last music pioneer Bob Marley, it seemed we had reached a point in the 20th century where there would be nothing new under the music sun. True, great artists were still creating phenomenal music, but no one anticipated the emergence of Nirvana, a Seattle based band that single-handedly opened doors for musicians to fully express emotions in sonic fury and passion.

Haiku Instrumental 1995

On a red-eye—
lights below:
such constellations to guide me home.

Inspired by *Music For Sleepwalking 4 (in G Major)* by *me* (Dave Muñoz), recorded live in San Francisco on December 28, 1995. In the mid 1990s, while working at City Storage on Townsend Street, San Francisco, I would bring in my electric keyboard and practice chord progressions on my lunch hour. After years of listening to Ambient music I didn't want to simply re-create the soundscapes of Brian Eno and Harold Budd, instead I wanted to create an ambient CD live with two electric keyboards and an acoustic piano. Steadfast to Eno's original philosophy of creating Ambient music as background sound, I performed my piece with very low recording levels and high restraint on dynamics. The CD was recorded in our apartment on 48th Avenue just off Ocean Beach, which added to the ambiance. I spent days preparing and before the recording session started, I told my wife Cristina that I was going to do a run-through first while she was making dinner. She didn't know that I had turned on the recording equipment so she went on chopping vegies and busying about. Towards the end of my practice-run session, amidst the ambient kitchen sounds, a co-worker calls and you can hear Cristina say as the music fades, "he's on his way." These ambient sounds thrilled me to no end! And so my rough-mix run-through became my original recording.

Haiku Song 1995

She said,
"I love you like flowers"—
then blows a dandelion clean away.

Inspired by "Fragile, Don't Crush" by The Softies from their album *It's Love*. I've always had a soft spot for the melancholic. The short-lived career of this lovely duet group of Rose Melberg and Jen Sbragia had its base in Portland, Oregon at a time when Northwestern America was at its most powerful with the *grunge* movement making waves. However, the two musicians turned their music arrangements and vocals into beautiful melodic songs filled with melancholy, wonder, falling in love, and heartache. "Fragile, Don't Crush," is so gentle it is enough to make one wish break-ups could only be this beautiful!

In late 1995 the duet released *It's Love* stripped down to bare instrumental necessities—in this case two guitars and duet vocals. This sound would be their amazing trademark! The Softies would release only two more CDs before slipping into the soft and gentle night.

Haiku Instrumental 1996

I think your near-sighted Cupid
shot me by mistake . . .
but I won't tell.

Inspired by "2nd Picture of Cristina" by me (Dave Muñoz), from the solo piano suite *Seven Pictures of Cristina*, part of my CD set entitled *The 1996 Basement Tapes*. In 1996 I placed all seven photographs of my wife on my piano to tell a story of her life through music. Some weeks later the 42-minute suite was complete and I laid down the tracks on tape. Between 1995 and 1996 two other works of mine were recorded: *Rhonda's Rondeau* (for my childhood friend), and a sonata in three movements entitled *The Santa Maria Sonata* for my dear friend and "soul-sister" Cristina Santa Maria-Graff. After the 1996 basement tapes were recorded I did nothing to them and stashed all three compositions in storage. But in 2007 I rediscovered them and remastered the tapes unto a CD.

Haiku Song 1996

Life's like
a magazine rack
with so many illusions to choose from.

Inspired by "Want To Buy Some Illusions" as sung by Marianne Faithfull. In 1996 Marianne released her incredible cabaret CD on RCA Victor. The CD entitled *20th Century Blues* featured cabaret songs from Kurt Weill, Noel Coward, and this one above by Fredrich Hollaender (an escapee from Nazi Germany). Singing cabaret was not new to Marianne nor to her many fans. So *20th Century Blues* turned out to be a "love letter" to her fans, such as my wife Cristina and me! In 1948 Hollaender composed this song for director Billy Wilder's film *A Foreign Affair*. The film star who sang the lead was the Blue Angel herself, Marlene Dietrich. "Marianne, may you long bask under Blue Angel's wing!"

Haiku Instrumental 1997

Off Key Largo
winds sound like a ghost—
wait, it's music from Cuba's coast.

Inspired by "Buena Vista Social Club" from the motion picture Soundtrack *Buena Vista Social Club*. The composition by Israel "Cachao" Lopez is a glorious theme-and-variation piece featuring Ry Cooder on guitar and national treasure Ruben Gonzales on piano. The film and CD soundtrack went on to win numerous awards. And hurray to artist Ry Cooder for his genius in seeking out and rediscovering these long-lost Cuban artists, and kudos to film director Wim Wenders for his compassionate touch!

Haiku Song 1997
5 Nonsensical Haikus Inspired By Radiohead's OK Computer

Airbag BURST!
Earth's a slinky little piggy
in a squealing tizzy.

Interstellar pies
land on horseshoe poles . . .
parasols in case it rains.

Karma accountant
in butterfly tent,
Ferris wheel around her scent.

I've gone too far backwards
leaving Earth's milky curd,
sing, sing widow bird!

Name engraved, brain wave,
close shave, bees take heed—
"You're coming to . . . breathe, just breathe."

Inspired by songs from Radiohead's seminal album *OK Computer*, using an array of sound-scape textures saluting as far back as Pink Floyd's *Dark Side of The Moon* and many other U.K. sonic artists of the time. *OK Computer* is an amazing achievement indeed. Here are the five *OK Computer* songs that inspired me to create my nonsensical haikus: "Airbag," "Paranoid Android," "Karma Police," "Subterranean Homesick Alien," "Exit Music (For a Film)."

Haiku Instrumental 1998
...*from here*...

"... I want to live here
where there's no fear,
where pain and sadness are light years ...

... I want to fix
houses, hospitals, horizons
and fill holes with hope ...

... bring sea creatures to skies,
babies to mothers' eyes,
watch the turning tides ...

... bring land creatures in from that tide,
raise them by hand
till time has them die ...

... plant plants, seed trees,
give them names and faces
and set them all free ...

... it's LIKE A NEW WORLD HERE
SHEDDING ITS SKIN!"
"... This is Houston ... get back in!"

Inspired by four instrumentals from the electronic-chillout genre-based CD *Moon Safari* by AIR French Band, consisting of multi-instrumentalists Nicolas Godin and Jean-Benoit Dunckel. Since the mid-1970s artists like Kraftwerk, Giorgio Moroder, Jean-Michel Jarre,

Klaus Schulze, Brian Eno, and lastly back to David Bowie's *LOW* album from 1977, all swam in an underground Electronica genre. But *Moon Safari* brought the genre out onto the mainstream floor . . . or should I say, the mainstream Universe. The tracks that inspired my haikus are as follows: "La Femme D'Argent;" "Talisman;" "Ce Matin La" and "Le Voyage De Penelope."

Haiku Song 1998

Rope stars on strings
if clouds are forming
guard earth like Perseus arming.

Inspired by "(Ghost) Riders In The Sky" from the CD *Johnny Cash and Willie Nelson, Live VH1 Storytellers*, produced by Rick Rubin. The song was originally composed by Stan Jones in 1948. The Storyteller Series took flight one memorable day in 1998 when the two good friends and Country Music giants sat down on stools with coffee, water, and hot chocolate. They had been dear friends since their younger days. In 1984 the two were part of a four Country Music super group called the Highwaymen, featuring Johnny Cash, Willie Nelson, Waylon Jennings, and Kris Kristofferson. I had been a huge fan of all four artists since my youth and to see Johnny and Willie meet together for this performance was (for me) like seeing what it would have been like to see John and Paul of the Beatles meet up again... But this is pure karmic metaphysics (another time and another place).

Haiku Instrumental 1999

You read me Earth's story
under shady trees . . .
sunlight breaks in between.

Inspired by "Trees" from my solo piano CD *Earth Works*. As I wrote in my CD liner notes, "*Earth Works* is a musical canvas of nature and our role in it. It was theoretically conceived in March of 1997 as fragments of bones in my head and, much like a paleozoology scientist, I worked on this composition by connecting pieces together as the months passed."

Haiku Song 1999

Let's dance like piñatas,
smash into each other
and rain candy.

Inspired by the song "Smooth" composed by Rob Thomas (lead singer of pop group Matchbox Twenty) and Itaal Shur, as performed by the iconic rock group Santana, featuring Thomas' sensual vocals and Carlos' ecstatic guitar. "Smooth" became a joyous phenomenon! It reigned as a hit through December of 1999 and ushered the song into the new millennium.

Of Journeys Home

Before words
and concepts on creation,
birds have utilized both
sun and moon
to guide them
to their homeward destination.

www.ingramcontent.com/pod-product-compliance
Lightning Source LLC
Chambersburg PA
CBHW051558010526
44118CB00023B/2741